F-101 VOODOO

 in detail & scale

Bert Kinzey

D & S
Vol. 21

COVERS ALL ONE-OH-WONDER VERSIONS!

TAB BOOKS Inc.
Blue Ridge Summit, PA 17294

Airlife Publishing Ltd.
England

This book is a product of Detail & Sccale, Inc., which has sole responsibility for its content and layout, except that all contributors are responsible for the security clearance and copyright release of all materials submitted. Published and distributed in the United States by TAB BOOKS, Inc., and in Great Britain and Europe by Airlife Publishing Ltd.

CONTRIBUTORS:

Doug Barbier
Lloyd Jones
Bill Slatton
Bruce Radebaugh
Ron Picciani
Arnold Swanberg
Bill Paul
The U.S. Air Force

Flightleader
Don Schmenk
Warren Munkasy
Norm Taylor
Charles Davenport
Daniel Soulaine
Jerry Geer
McDonnell Douglas

Detail & Scale expresses a special thanks to Peggy Young and Bill Paul of the Robins AFB Museum. Bill Paul patiently assisted through three trips to photograph two F-101Bs and one F-101F that remain at Robins AFB. A number of the photographs that appear in this book were made possible through his efforts.

SECOND EDITION
SECOND PRINTING

Published in United States by

TAB BOOKS Inc.
Blue Ridge Summit, PA 17294

Library of Congress Cataloging in Publication Data:

Kinzey, Bert.
F-101.
(Detail and scale ; vol. 21)
1. Voodoo (Jet fighter plane) I. Title.
UG1242.F5K536 1986 358.4'3
85-27707
ISBN 0-8306-8131-0 (pbk.)

Published in Great Britain by
Airlife Publishing Ltd.
7 St. John's Hill
Shrewsbury, 5Y1 1JE

British Library Cataloging in Publication Data:

The F-101.—(Detail and scale series; 21)
   1. McDonnell Douglas airplanes—History
      I. Series
      623.74'64 UG1242.F5

   ISBN 0-85368-871-0

Questions regarding the content of this book should be addressed to:

Reader Inquiry Branch
Editorial Department
TAB BOOKS Inc.
Blue Ridge Summit, PA 17294

FRONT COVER: Early F-101B in a test flight without the canopy.   (Taylor)

REAR COVER: Front instrument panel in an F-101B.

INTRODUCTION

This head-on view shows details of the intakes, landing gear, and canopy on an early F-101B. Note the strakes on either side of the weapons bay, and the refrigeration air intake slot just to the left of the nose gear (to the right in the photo). This was later replaced with a scoop on most F-101Bs. This aircraft is F-101B-50-MC, 56-0240, and was photographed at McEntire ANGB, South Carolina, in 1960. *(Taylor collection)*

The F-101 Voodoo in Detail & Scale, as originally published, marked a last for Detail & Scale, Inc.. It was the last book released prior to contracting with Aero Publishers for them to print and distribute the Detail & Scale Series. Thus, it became the last title for which Detail & Scale, Inc., handled not only the production end, but all distribution for the book as well. That small, thirty-six page book on the Voodoo sold quite well, but really was not large enough to cover the subject as thoroughly as we would have liked.

This new edition of the F-101 Voodoo in Detail & Scale is almost an entirely new book, and, just as the first edition marked a last, this new edition is an important first. This is the first title to be released through a new agreement with TAB BOOKS, Inc. We believe that through TAB, we will continue to improve and expand the Detail & Scale Series to an even greater extent than before.

Being twice as large as the original edition, this book offers the most detailed look yet at McDonnell's One-Oh-Wonder. We have been able to include many additional detailed photographs, almost all of which were taken specifically for this publication. For example, to our knowledge, this is the only publication to provide photographs of the radar antenna in the F-101B. Cockpit photos are included for the RF-101A/C, F-101B, and F-101F, while

flight manual drawings provide details of the F-101A/C cockpit.

While emphasis is placed on the most popular of the Voodoo variants, the F-101B, coverage is not limited to only the two seat version. Details of the F-101A/C, RF-101A/C, and the reconnaissance conversions, the RF-101B, -G, and -H are also provided. A developmental history that also covers the XF-88 Voodoo is included, as is background information on each version. But this is kept to a minimum in order to include as many of the detailed photographs as possible. These photos were selected from over twelve-hundred from our files and from other contributors.

For the scale modeler, the Modeler's Section covers the Voodoo kits, from the F-88 by Lindberg, dating back to the 1950s, to the newly released Monogram F-101B, thus spanning over thirty years of model making.

A number of contributors provided materials for this publication, and their names are listed on the previous page. Their efforts are sincerely appreciated. A special thanks goes to Peggy Young and Bill Paul of the Robins AFB museum, and to Bruce Radebaugh at Robins AFB. Through their efforts, access was gained to obtain photographs of three F-101s that remain at Robins AFB.

DEVELOPMENTAL HISTORY

The first prototype of the XF-88, 46525, is shown late in the experimental program with small afterburners added.
(McDonnell Douglas)

The F-101 traces its lineage back to the XF-88, a McDonnell design for a "penetration fighter" to escort bombers deep into enemy territory. That design, known as Model 36W at McDonnell, was in response to a USAAF requirement, issued on August 28, 1945. On June 20, 1946, a contract was issued for two XF-88s, but structural design changes caused delays in the program.

Following the tradition of giving McDonnell fighters names from the realms of spooks and witchery (Phantom, Banshee, Demon, and Goblin having already been used)

The first XF-88 Voodoo is shown at its rollout from the McDonnell plant. It was originally planned for the aircraft to have straight wings, but this was changed to a thirty-five degree sweep back at 25% chord. This aircraft first flew on October 20, 1948. *(McDonnell Douglas)*

the new XF-88 was dubbed Voodoo, and began on the drawing boards in a straight wing configuration, not unlike the F2H Banshee. Another proposal had jet engines on the wing tips, but when it reached the hardware stage, the XF-88 had a wing with a sweep back of thirty-five degrees, a conventional swept tailplane, and two J34-WE-13 engines, each producing 3000 pounds of thrust. The aircraft looked quite advanced for its day, and had split flaps, leading edge flaps, speed brakes, and boundary layer fences on the wings. Plans to include large, 350 gallon tip tanks were abandoned. The aircraft had a span of 39 feet 8 inches, a length of 54 feet 2 inches, and a height of 17 feet 3 inches. The wing area was 350 square feet. Empty weight was 12,140 pounds, and maximum take-off weight was 23,100 pounds.

The first prototype (46-525) was rolled-out on October 11, 1948, and first flown on October 20th. The aircraft reached a top speed of 641 miles per hour, and could exceed the speed of sound in a dive.

The second XF-88 (46-526) made its first flight on April 26, 1949, being fitted with short thirty-inch afterburners in June of that year. With the afterburners, the Voodoo was redesignated XF-88A, and later the afterburners were added to the first prototype. It is interesting to note that these afterburners were of a McDonnell design. Engine manufacturers, to include Westinghouse, seemed unwilling to develop an afterburner. McDonnell's engineers came up with what was truly an exceptional and effective afterburner that even featured a multi-flap, variable nozzle. With the afterburner, available thrust was increased to 3600 pounds, and top speed exceeded 700 miles per hour.

The first prototype was fitted with an Allison XF-35A turbo-prop engine. Several thin blade designs, capable of turning supersonic tip speeds, were tried during this test program. (McDonnell Douglas)

Testing of the XF-88 was remarkably free of problems, and McDonnell submitted a proposal to build both fighter and reconnaissance versions. In June 1950, the Air Force evaluated the Voodoo against Lockheed's XF-90 and North American's XF-93. Although the XF-88 was declared the winner, the program was soon cancelled. This was not due to problems with the aircraft itself, but to two other reasons. First, early jet engines had very high fuel consumption, and simply could not provide the long range capability required of a penetration fighter, and have acceptable combat performance at the same time. The second factor causing cancellation of the XF-88 program was the ever-present monetary constraints placed on military spending, particularly during peacetime. Budget priorities went first to the concept of nuclear deterrance in the form of bombs and bombers, and secondly to fighter-interceptors to protect American skies from the enemy's bombs and bombers. Therefore the F-86D interceptor got the funds and the XF-88 did not.

Because of the overall success of the design and test program, the two XF-88As were placed in storage, rather than being scrapped. In the meantime, SAC would rely on the F-84E to escort its bombers, with the swept wing F-84F replacing it as the new version became available.

But as so often proves to be the case, combat, this time

in Korea, dramatized the shortcomings of trying to make-do with less than adequate equipment. Soviet-built fighters easily scored against American bombers, and the F-84 was outclassed by the MiG-15. What good is nuclear deterrence if the bombers that are to deliver the bombs are sitting ducks? The Air Force wanted a better long range penetration fighter, and initiated both short range and long range programs to solve the problem.

The second prototype, XF-88, 46526 is shown here in its final configuration. After the short afterburners were added, and also retrofitted to the first prototype, the designation was changed to XF-88A. Note the installation of six 20 mm cannon. (McDonnell Douglas)

The first F-101A Voodoo is shown with the second XF-88 prototype in the McDonnell plant. Similarities, as well as differences between the two designs, can be seen in this photo. F3H Demons and two more F-101s can be seen in the background.
(Taylor collection)

In one program, the first XF-88 prototype was recalled from storage, and fitted with an Allison XT-38A turbo-prop engine in addition to its two jet engines. It was first flown in this "tri-motor" configuration on April 14, 1953, and as such, was designated XF-88B. Various blade designs were tested that could produce supersonic tip speeds, and the idea was to give the fighter more range with the turbo-prop than could be provided by the thirsty jets. The jets would be used to provide the combat performance.

Several other aircraft, ranging from the F-84 to the B-17, served as test beds for turbo-prop engines, but in the final analysis, the turbo-prop proved unsatisfactory, and the Air Force would have to find another way to escort its bombers to their targets. While the flying days of the XF-88 came to an end, it already had become a factor of considerable significance in another effort to solve the problem of developing a suitable penetration fighter.

Although the Air Force had cancelled the XF-88 program, and had planned to use existing F-84s as escort

fighters, SAC was not happy with the decision. They wanted a long range fighter, capable of escorting their new B-36, and generally felt that the F-84 was unsatisfactory as a bomber escort. The truth of this belief was certainly evident in the skies over Korea. Therefore, in January 1951, SAC outlined its own minimum requirements for a long range penetration fighter. The following month General Operational Requirements (GOR) 101 was published, and in May several proposals from the industry were considered. These included three submissions from Republic, two versions of the F-84F and the F-91, an improved Northrop F-89, North American's F-93, Lockheed's F-90 and F-94, and a redesigned and improved XF-88 from McDonnell. From this field, the McDonnell design was the clear winner, partly due to the previous success with the XF-88, and also because the Air Force believed that the program would be relatively low risk since the aircraft was essentially a modified form of a proven design.

In October 1951, a production "go-ahead" was issued. It is no coincidence that this was the same month that B-29s

The first F-101A-1-MC, 53-2418, is seen here with its name painted on the nose. The Voodoo's clean lines and sleek design are clearly evident, and seem to foreshadow the speed that this large fighter was to attain in its operational service.

(McDonnell Douglas)

suffered great losses in Korea. Because of the considerable changes made to the XF-88 design, the designation was changed to F-101 in November 1951. However, the name of Voodoo was retained.

In early 1952, McDonnell and the Air Force began working out design details, which proved to be a lengthy process. The requirements now called for a dual role "strategic fighter," one that could not only escort the bombers and engage in air-to-air combat to protect them, but could also perform the mission of a nuclear fighter-bomber.

The first delivery of an F-101A was made in August 1954, and it made its first flight on September 29. During the half-hour flight, it broke through the speed of sound in a dive. The following month, the Air Force lifted a previous production hold order (issued in May 1954), so that production and flight testing could proceed.

Several problems were discovered during testing, two of which are noteworthy. One was a compressor stall problem that was corrected by changing the intake duct design. The second and more difficult problem was a tendency for the aircraft to pitch-up at high angles of attack. The XF-88 had its horizontal tail surfaces mounted low on the vertical fin, but one of the design changes in the F-101 was a T tail configuration. At high angles of attack, the wing was so disturbing and blocking the air flow over the horizontal tail that it lost lift, resulting in a severe nose pitch-up. This could then cause the plane to go into a spin. From a design standpoint, there was not much to be done about the pitch-up problem. A pitch-up device, known as an active inhibitor, was installed, and it sounded a warning horn to the pilot if a pitch-up condition was approached. However, the "solution," simply put, was to fly the Voodoo strictly "by the book". Failure to do so, particularly at supersonic speeds, when the aircraft gave little or no warning of an approaching pitch-up condition, would result in a rather harrowing flying experience that was not always recovered from successfully.

Experiments were carried out to increase the F-101's range to the maximum in order to permit it to escort long-range bombers. Here 53-2427 carries a huge weapons/fuel pod which had a capacity of 703 gallons of fuel. This configuration resulted in a gross take-off weight of nearly 50,000 pounds.

(McDonnell Douglas via Taylor)

The RF-101A/C became the tactical reconnaissance workhorse of the Air Force, and saw extensive use in Vietnam. Cameras were carried in an elongated angular nose.
(Taylor collection)

While flight testing continued, McDonnell's production line continued to turn out aircraft, with both the fighter version and a reconnaissance RF-101A being built. But as testing and evaluation progressed, over 2000 engineering improvements and design changes were incorporated, and it became a tremendous job just to retrofit these into existing aircraft. Most significant was the fact that the first F-101s and RF-101s were only built to withstand 6.33Gs, whereas the GOR called for 7.33Gs. When it became apparent that it would not be practical to retrofit all of the changes necessary to bring the 6.33G airframes up to the 7.33G standards, it was decided to leave the 6.33G aircraft as such, designating them F-101As and RF-101As for the fighter and reconnaissance versions respectively.

It was May 2, 1957, before the first F-101A was accepted into the operational inventory, and only fifty of the seventy-seven built made it into Air Force squadrons. The RF-101A and the subsequent RF-101C fared much better than the

strategic fighter versions. But it was another variant that was to become the most successful of all of the Voodoo models. This was the two-seat F-101B that was designed to be an interceptor to shoot bombers down rather than protect them. Thus it became an ironic twist of fate that saw the most widely used version of the F-101 employed in a role that was exactly the opposite for which the basic design was originally intended.

Several factors influenced the development of an interceptor version of the F-101. At a time when the Soviets were causing alarm by exploding a thermonuclear bomb, the Air Force's plans to develop an "ultimate" interceptor (F-106), by first building an "interim" interceptor (F-102), were falling on hard times, being plagued with serious delays. The F-86D, then the best interceptor in service, lacked the speed, range, and sophistication the Air Defense Command (ADC) thought necessary to do the job of defending America from the Soviet bomber threat.

The most widely produced version of the Voodoo was the two-seat F-101B interceptor. This is an early F-101B, as evidenced by the cooling slot on the engine fairing. This was shortly replaced with a rather large scoop. It is interesting to note that the TAC insignia is painted on the tail. Voodoo interceptors were assigned to ADC, and ADC did not become a part of TAC until all but a very few F-101Bs were retired from service. (Taylor collection)

In October 1952, ADC suggested that the fast and long ranged F-101 could be modified to fit the interceptor role. But Air Force Headquarters argued against the idea, reasoning that it was too expensive to fund both Convair's F-102/F-106 program and another new interceptor program at the same time. The Air Force argued that it would be more cost effective and simple to increase the number of F-86Ds, while putting pressure on Convair to get the F-102 and the F-106 into service. Cost effective - yes, but the question remained, how operationally effective would it be?

ADC persisted, and in late 1953, the Air Force consented to soliciting proposals from the industry for an interceptor that could be developed quickly to fill the gap until Convair could get the F-102, and eventually the F-106, ready for operational service. North American proposed an interceptor version of the Super Sabre. Northrop offered an improved F-89, but McDonnell's F-101 was considered to have the best potential. However, in May 1954, when this decision was made, there was no immediate go-ahead order.

In March 1955, contractural arrangements were finally made for McDonnell to begin work on an interceptor version that was later designated F-101B in August of that year. But a lengthy production hold delayed the first flight of the F-101B until March 27, 1957. In the meantime, much work was dedicated to finding an acceptable fire control system and weapons for that system to control. McDonnell began with a single-seat design, but ultimately the Air Force opted for a two-seat configuration, with the rear seat being occupied by a "radar observer" to operate the MG-13 fire control system that was eventually chosen for the F-101B. Originally, the aircraft was to be armed only with rockets like the F-86D and F-89D. Next came a combination of rockets and three Falcon missiles, but finally a combination of two IR guided Falcons and two unguided, but nuclear capable, AIR-2A Genies was selected. These would be carried on a rotary weapons door under the fuselage. The gun armament of the F-101A/C was deleted.

After two years of testing, the F-101B entered operational service in January 1959. Production continued through March 1961, with 480 F-101Bs and dual-control F-101Fs being accepted.

As each version of the Voodoo is covered on the following pages, more specific information on each version will be presented. The Voodoo program as a whole enjoyed amazing longevity. The first XF-88 flew in 1948, and it was not until 1984 that the last CF-101Bs were retired from service.

F-101 DETAILS

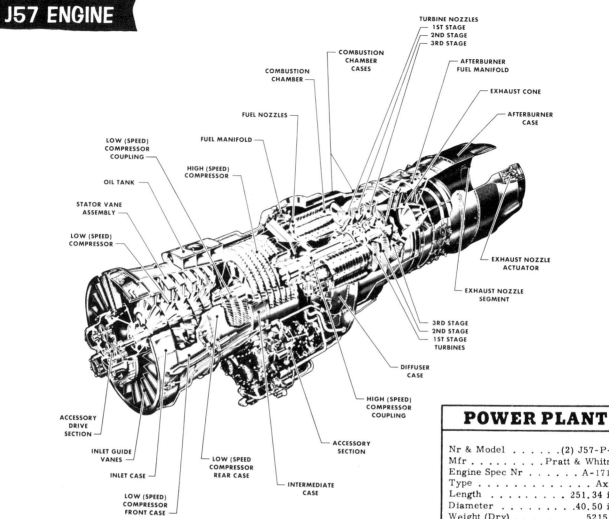

TURBINE NOZZLES
1ST STAGE
2ND STAGE
3RD STAGE

COMBUSTION CHAMBER CASES

COMBUSTION CHAMBER

AFTERBURNER FUEL MANIFOLD

EXHAUST CONE

AFTERBURNER CASE

FUEL NOZZLES

FUEL MANIFOLD

LOW (SPEED) COMPRESSOR COUPLING

HIGH (SPEED) COMPRESSOR

OIL TANK

STATOR VANE ASSEMBLY

LOW (SPEED) COMPRESSOR

EXHAUST NOZZLE ACTUATOR

EXHAUST NOZZLE SEGMENT

3RD STAGE
2ND STAGE
1ST STAGE
TURBINES

DIFFUSER CASE

HIGH (SPEED) COMPRESSOR COUPLING

ACCESSORY DRIVE SECTION

INLET GUIDE VANES

INLET CASE

LOW (SPEED) COMPRESSOR REAR CASE

ACCESSORY SECTION

INTERMEDIATE CASE

LOW (SPEED) COMPRESSOR FRONT CASE

POWER PLANT

Nr & Model . . . . . . (2) J57-P-55
Mfr . . . . Pratt & Whitney
Engine Spec Nr A-1718D
Type . . . . Axial
Length . . . . 251.34 in.
Diameter . . . . .40.50 in.
Weight (Dry) . . . . 5215 lb
Tail Pipe . . . . . . Two Position
C-D Nozzle
Augmentation . . . . . Afterburner

POWER PLANT

Nr & Model . . . . (2) J57-P-13
Mfr . . . . Pratt & Whitney
Engine Spec. Nr A-1688D
Type . . . . Axial
Length . . . . 211.0"
Diameter . . . . 40.3"
Weight (Dry) . . . . 5025 lb
Tail Pipe . . . . Two-Position
Augmentation . . . . . Afterburning

ENGINE RATINGS

S.L. Static   LB - RPM - MIN

Max: *15,000 - 6150/9900 -   5

Mil: 10,200 - 6150/9900 - 30

Nor: 8700 - 5900/9650 - Cont

*With afterburner operating

First figure represents the RPM of the low pressure spool while the second that of the high pressure spool.

ENGINE RATINGS

S.L.S.   LB - †RPM - MIN

Max: *16,900 - 6400/10,070 - 5

Mil: 10,700 - 6350/10,070 - 30

Nor: 9150 - 6050/9750 - Cont

* With afterburner operating

† First figure represents the RPM of the low pressure spool while the second that of the high pressure spool.

The J-57 engine powered all versions of the F-101. However there were some differences. The F-101B used the J57-P-55 with a larger afterburner and more power. All other versions used a -13 version of the engine. Data for both versions of the engine is given above. The J-57 engine also powered the F-100 and F-102 fighters as well as many other aircraft ranging up to the B-52.

NOSE LANDING GEAR DETAIL

These three photos show the nose landing gear from three different angles. Note the wheel design in the photo at left, while the center photo shows the spring and part of the retracting strut. At right, the nose gear is seen from behind, with details of the steering rams clearly shown.

(Left author, center and right Davenport)

At left is the nose gear from the front showing the two large lights. The retracting strut is also in evidence. The center photo shows the nose gear well looking aft, and the photo on the right is looking forward. Note the arms that open and close the gear doors.

(All photos, Davenport)

MAIN LANDING GEAR DETAIL

These three photos show details of the main landing gear used on all single seat F-101s, and the very first F-101Bs. There are three doors connected to the main strut. The top door stays parallel to the wing when open, and the other doors are flat, covering the strut and tire. Note that the bottom door is flat, as seen in the front view.

(Left author, center and right Davenport)

The heavier two-seat F-101B was fitted with a wider and larger main gear wheel as seen in these three photos. In order to accommodate these larger tires, bulges were added to the lower gear door and the wing just aft of the wheel well. The bulged lower gear door is evident in these photos, and can be compared to the flat door in the photos above.

(Left author, center and right Davenport)

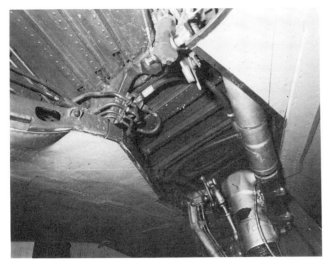
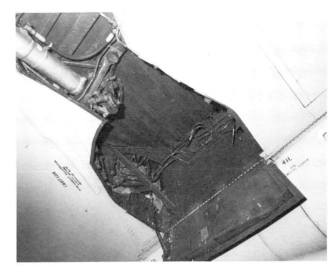

These two photos show details of the left main gear well. As with the nose gear well, the interiors of the main gear wells were painted chromate green, and the insides of the doors were gloss red.　(Both Davenport)

At left is the left main gear well looking forward, and at right is the same well looking aft. This is an F-101B as evidenced by the bulge that is seen in the wing and gear well in the photo at right.　(Both Davenport)

The photo at left shows the inner main gear door on the right main gear well of an F-101B. The arm that opens and closes the door can be seen at the forward end of the door. At right is a close-up of the inside of the right main wheel on an F-101B.

EJECTION SEAT DETAIL

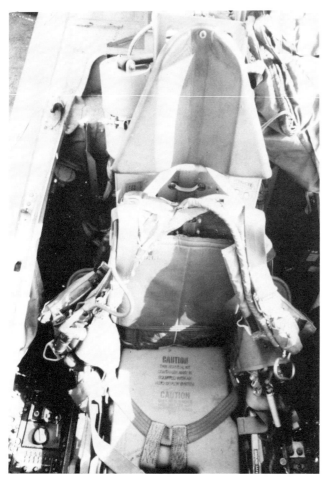

A fully packed seat, complete with parachute, is shown in the photo at left. The seat is in an RF-101C. At right is the front seat in an F-101B, and the parachute pack is not present. Note the padded head rest.

Ejection seat in the front cockpit.

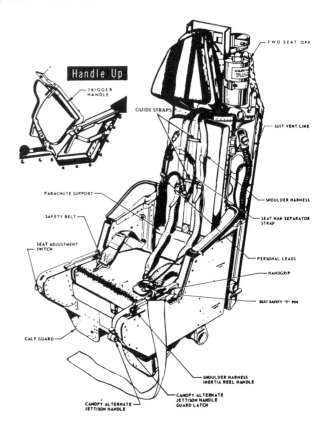

F-101A & F-101C TACTICAL FIGHTER

The first F-101A is shown again during its initial testing. Note the covers over the gun fairings. (McDonnell Douglas)

On September 29, 1954, the F-101A made its first flight just as SAC cancelled its requirements for the aircraft. What should have been obvious all along was finally realized and admitted. It was just not possible to build a fighter that could escort a bomber on a 10,000 mile trip. The Voodoo was the largest and heaviest fighter ever built, with an outstanding range for a fighter. Its ferry range was 2186 miles, with a combat radius of 677 miles, less than one-quarter of what the B-36 could do. Therefore the F-101 was never to perform the primary mission for which it was designed, that of escorting bombers, and it is just as well that it never had to. When the F-101 became operational, the Societ interceptor force was made up mostly of MiG-19s, MiG-17s, and a few MiG-15s. The MiG-21 entered the inventory while the F-101 was in service. These MiGs would have been the fighters that the F-101 would have had to engage to protect the bombers. The MiGs were all light-weight, highly maneuverable, and deployed in large numbers. It takes little imagination to realize what kind of air battle the relatively huge and cumbersome Voodoo would have found itself in with so many MiGs swarming around like gnats.

Dispite SAC's cancellation of its requirements for a long range escort fighter, work continued on the Voodoo, but not without a lot of problems. There were engine problems, armament problems, aerodynamic and structural problems, not all of which were solved. Structurally, the GOR required a 7.33G airframe, but the first aircraft were built to withstand only 6.33Gs, and the point at which the change to the stronger structure would be used kept getting pushed further and further down the production line. Although it was originally planned for the 6.33G aircraft to be brought up to 7.33G standards, it was finally realized that this was going to be impossible. Therefore it was decided that the 6.33G aircraft would be designated F-101As, and the 7.33G aircraft received the F-101C designation.

Although SAC had decided it did not want the F-101 after all, and despite the problems, there were some positive points in the F-101s favor. It was the hottest, fastest fighter in the sky, and on December 12, 1957, a pre-production F-101A, piloted by Major Adrain Drew, set a world speed record of 1207.3 mph at Edwards AFB. During the record run, the aircraft was fitted with the larger after-burners that became standard on the F-101B/F. The aircraft also had great range, and good avionics for its day, to include a dual mode radar, M-1 Toss Bombing System, and a Low Altitude Bombing System (LABS). The aircraft could also be in-flight refueled by both the probe and drogue system and the high speed boom.

Both the F-101A and F-101C carried four M-39 cannon aimed through a K-19 gunsight. Often, one of the right side guns was deleted and replaced with navigation equipment. A number of sources report that the F-101A/C also carried three Falcon missiles and two retractable packs carrying 2.75 inch rockets. The fact is that these provisions were planned for in the F-101 design, but were deleted and did not make it to the production stage. Lastly, there was a centerline hardpoint on which a nuclear or conventional bomb could be carried, but for all practical purposes, the

This cutaway drawing shows many of the internal details of the F-101A/C. Locations of the fuselage fuel cells, guns, and ammunition stowage are all shown.
(McDonnell Douglas)

F-101A/C was a nuclear fighter-bomber only.

Even though SAC decided it did not want the Voodoo, it was SAC's 27th Strategic Fighter Wing (SFW) that received the first operational F-101A on May 2, 1957. But SAC quickly turned the Wing and its aircraft over to TAC on July 1, 1957. The 27th SFW became the 27th Fighter-Bomber Wing (FBW), but it remained at Bergstrom AFB. The unit began training for the only mission the aircraft could perform, that of all-weather, low-level, nuclear strike.

The F-101C began to replace the F-101A in the 27th FBW in September 1957. The F-101As were transferred to the 81st TFW in England. Later, the 81st would also receive some F-101Cs, but since only forty-seven -C models were built, there were not enough to fully equip both the 27th FBW and 81st TFW. Therefore, the 81st TFW continued to operate both versions until they were replaced in 1966 by another McDonnell product, the F-4C. At that time, twenty-nine of the remaining F-101As were converted to RF-101Gs, while thirty-two F-101Cs became RF-101Hs. (See pages 25 and 26.)

Plagued with problems during its development, the fastest, largest, and heaviest fighter ever built up to that time was given away by SAC, and was received less than enthusiastically by TAC. This was because the aircraft, for all practical purposes, could only deliver nuclear weapons, not conventional ones, and required basing at a major facility due to its weight and ground support requirements. But the operational service life was at least moderately successful. A number of record-setting flights were made, and they satisfactorily performed their important mission in the less-than-perfect weather in England. However, it must be admitted that it was the RF-101A/C, and to an even greater extent, the F-101B, that proved the real worth of the Voodoo and made the design a success for both McDonnell and the Air Force.

The first F-101A shown in flight.
(McDonnell Douglas)

F-101A-30-MC, 54-1462, of the 91st TFS, photographed at Bentwaters Air Base, May 15, 1960.　　*(Taylor collection)*

F-101C-20-MC, 54-1487, of the 81st TFW as it appeared in October 1965. This was the second F-101C built.
(Taylor collection)

F-101C-45-MC, 56-0009, pictured at Bentwaters, England, on September 18, 1965.　　*(Taylor collection)*

F-101A/C DETAILS

Above: Left side of the nose of an F-101A showing the cannon armament. (Taylor collection)

Right: Right side with the cannon cover open. Quite often one of the right side cannon was removed and replaced with a TACAN receiver as seen here. (Taylor collection)

This close-up of the right side of the nose shows the cannon fairings, radome, pitot tube, and windscreen to good effect. The aircraft is F-101C, 56-0006, assigned to the 81st TFW. As was the case with many F-101As and -Cs, the aircraft is painted silver overall to help prevent corrosion. (Taylor collection)

Each engine fairing had a cooling slot to cool the aft engine bay. This slot was originally on the F-101B, but was replaced with large scoops in the same location.

F-101A/C COCKPIT DETAIL

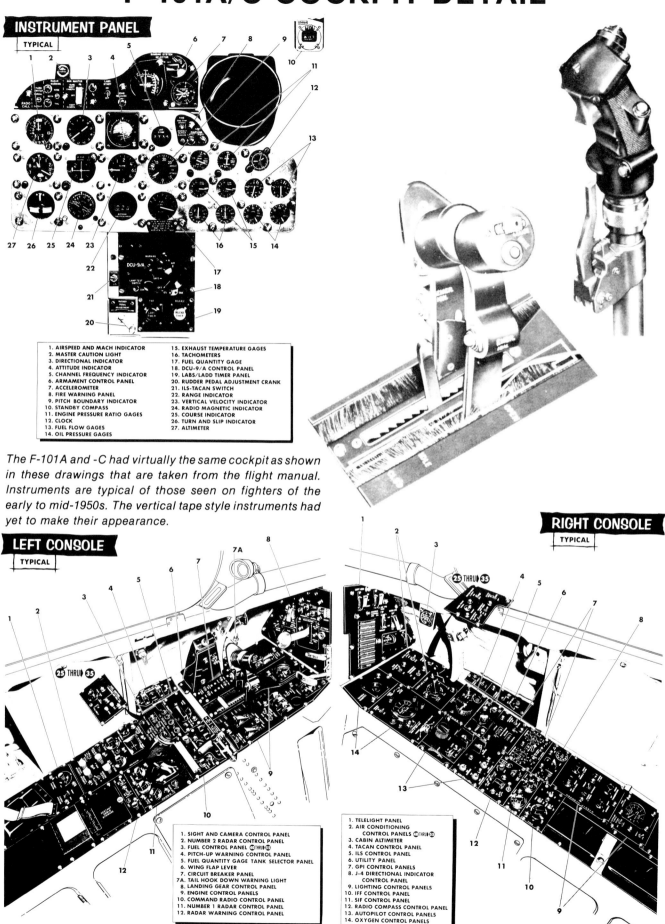

INSTRUMENT PANEL TYPICAL

1. AIRSPEED AND MACH INDICATOR
2. MASTER CAUTION LIGHT
3. DIRECTIONAL INDICATOR
4. ATTITUDE INDICATOR
5. CHANNEL FREQUENCY INDICATOR
6. ARMAMENT CONTROL PANEL
7. ACCELEROMETER
8. FIRE WARNING PANEL
9. PITCH BOUNDARY INDICATOR
10. STANDBY COMPASS
11. ENGINE PRESSURE RATIO GAGES
12. CLOCK
13. FUEL FLOW GAGES
14. OIL PRESSURE GAGES
15. EXHAUST TEMPERATURE GAGES
16. TACHOMETERS
17. FUEL QUANTITY GAGE
18. DCU-9/A CONTROL PANEL
19. LABS/LADD TIMER PANEL
20. RUDDER PEDAL ADJUSTMENT CRANK
21. ILS-TACAN SWITCH
22. RANGE INDICATOR
23. VERTICAL VELOCITY INDICATOR
24. RADIO MAGNETIC INDICATOR
25. COURSE INDICATOR
26. TURN AND SLIP INDICATOR
27. ALTIMETER

The F-101A and -C had virtually the same cockpit as shown in these drawings that are taken from the flight manual. Instruments are typical of those seen on fighters of the early to mid-1950s. The vertical tape style instruments had yet to make their appearance.

LEFT CONSOLE TYPICAL

1. SIGHT AND CAMERA CONTROL PANEL
2. NUMBER 2 RADAR CONTROL PANEL
3. FUEL CONTROL PANEL 20 THRU 33
4. PITCH-UP WARNING CONTROL PANEL
5. FUEL QUANTITY GAGE TANK SELECTOR PANEL
6. WING FLAP LEVER
7. CIRCUIT BREAKER PANEL
7A. TAIL HOOK DOWN WARNING LIGHT
8. LANDING GEAR CONTROL PANEL
9. ENGINE CONTROL PANELS
10. COMMAND RADIO CONTROL PANEL
11. NUMBER 1 RADAR CONTROL PANEL
12. RADAR WARNING CONTROL PANEL

RIGHT CONSOLE TYPICAL

1. TELELIGHT PANEL
2. AIR CONDITIONING CONTROL PANELS 20 THRU 33
3. CABIN ALTIMETER
4. TACAN CONTROL PANEL
5. ILS CONTROL PANEL
6. UTILITY PANEL
7. GPI CONTROL PANELS
8. J-4 DIRECTIONAL INDICATOR CONTROL PANEL
9. LIGHTING CONTROL PANELS
10. IFF CONTROL PANEL
11. SIF CONTROL PANEL
12. RADIO COMPASS CONTROL PANEL
13. AUTOPILOT CONTROL PANELS
14. OXYGEN CONTROL PANELS

RF-101A & RF-101C

The first F-101 version to make the headlines was the RF-101A/C when it provided reconnaissance during the Cuban "Missile Crisis." It later provided valuable tactical reconnaissance in Vietnam. *(Taylor collection)*

This overhead view of an RF-101A reveals the ever-present wing walkways, common to all Voodoos. There are no inner wing "fences" on this early aircraft. *(Taylor collection)*

There was very little difference between the RF-101s and their fighter counterparts. The RFs had a lengthened angular nose that housed the camera equipment instead of guns, and two cameras were also carried behind the pilot. The recon nose increased the fuselage length almost two feet, but otherwise, there was little change from the fighter design. The RF-101s even retained the nuclear delivery capability of the fighters.

The first YRF-101A made its maiden flight in May 1954, followed by the second prototype a month later. The first production aircraft flew for the first time in June 1956. Beginning with the fourth production aircraft, fuel tank capacity was supplemented with the addition of a seventy-five gallon tank in each wing. The RF-101A entered service on May 6, 1957, being assigned to the 363rd TRW at Shaw AFB.

The RF-101C first flew on July 12, 1957, and became operational with the 432nd TRW later that year. Production continued through March 1959.

It would be safe to say that the RF-101s were welcomed into service more than the fighters were. The Air Force scratched plans for the RF-104 and RF-105 in favor of the Voodoo, and the RF-101C was to become the workhorse of TAC's tactical reconnaissance squadrons for well over a decade. The aircraft made overflights of Cuba during the "Missile Crisis" in 1962, and were used in Vietnam from 1961 to 1970.

Although the recon Voodoos had some problems (the fleet was grounded for a week in January 1959 because of

All Voodoos suffered corrosion problems, and therefore were painted for protection. Prior to the time the SEA camouflage scheme was specified, RF-101s were painted in other colors. The photos on this page show three examples. Above is RF-101A-30-MC, 54-1513, assigned to the 29th TFS, 363rd TRW, based at Shaw AFB, South Carolina. When this photo was taken, the aircraft was in Alaska for exercise "Polar Siege" in January 1964. The entire aircraft is flat black. All lettering is red, and the band around the nose is white. (Taylor)

Above: Also photographed in Alaska, RF-101A-30-MC, 54-1512, is shown in overall ADC gray. The fuel tanks are painted silver, and the buzz number can be seen above them on the engine fairing. (Taylor)

Right: This photo shows an early attempt to paint the RF-101 as much for camouflage as for corrosion protection. Greens were painted in an irregular pattern over the upper surfaces. The large national insignias are still being used. This photo was taken at Danang Air Base, Vietnam, and the aircraft is RF-101C-55-MC, 56-0203. (Taylor collection)

collapsing main gear, and were later grounded again for hydraulic failures) there were relatively few problems with the aircraft during operational service when compared to other aircraft of similar complexity. All Voodoos suffered skin corrosion, the RFs being no exception. But the real deficiency was caused by a inadequate camera equipment, and a shortage of what equipment that was available. In 1962, a major modernization program was begun to upgrade the capabilities, and a photo flash cartridge pod provided a limited night capability. But providing sufficient quantities of quality recon equipment was an ongoing effort of a major magnitude.

Like their fighting counsins, recon Voodoos were produced under two designations, RF-101A and RF-101C. Again, the difference between the two was the beefed-up internal structure of the -C to a 7.33G specification whereas the -A was only a 6.33G airframe. Only thirty-five RF-101As were built before giving way to the RF-101C. Originally, the contract called for seventy RF-101Cs, but with the lack of interest demonstrated for the fighter version, the last ninety-six F-101Cs were built as RF-101Cs, bringing the total built to 166.

Several notable milestones highlighted the career of the RF-101, the most significant of which was the well documented "Operation Sun Run." This was a successful transcontinental record-breaking speed run involving six RF-101Cs. Flights were made from Ontario IAP, California, to NAS Floyd Bennett, New York. Then the run was reversed. The best total time was six hours, forty-six minutes and thirty-six seconds, recorded by Captain Robert Sweet.

On April 15, 1959, another RF-101C set a new world speed record of 816.279 miles per hour over a 500 kilometer closed circuit course.

RF-101Cs began being transferred to the Air National Guard in 1969 as RF-4Cs replaced them in active squadrons. They served in the Guard with RF-101Gs, -Hs, and two-seat RF-101Bs until final phaseout in January 1979. The last RF-101C to fly is pictured on page 34.

RF-101A/C CAMERA BAYS

A publicity shot shows the open camera bays on RF-101C-50-MC, 56-0187, with the different cameras that can be carried displayed in front of the aircraft. The aircraft is painted silver. (USAF via Taylor)

Head-on view showing the forward looking camera with the nose cover open. (USAF via Taylor)

Left camera bay detail with the left oblique camera removed.

Right camera bay with cameras in place. The vertical camera can be seen at the forward end of the bay.

These two views show the camera locations under the nose of the RF-101A/C.

RF-101A/C DETAILS

Open access panels on either side of the nose.

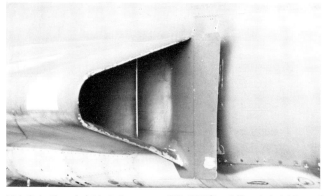

At left is the right intake on an RF-101C, while at right is a view looking back to the engine through the left intake. Note the hole in the nose of the cone.

Wing tip light detail.

Above: Afterburner cans on an RF-101C. These are the smaller burner cans used on all single seat versions of the F-101.

Right: Tail detail showing the deeper "keel" between the engines that was standard on single seat F-101s.

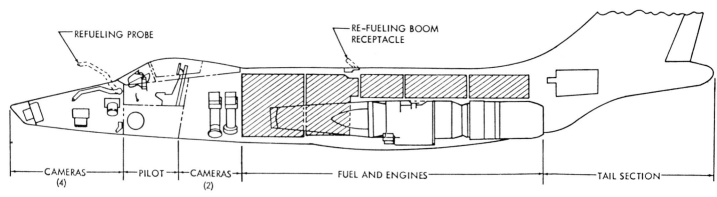

REFUELING PROBE

RE-FUELING BOOM RECEPTACLE

CAMERAS (4) — PILOT — CAMERAS (2) — FUEL AND ENGINES — TAIL SECTION

RECON CONVERSIONS

RF-101H-40-MC, 54-1486, of the 165th TRS, Kentucky ANG. The photo was taken at Elmendorf AFB, Alaska, on August 26, 1968, during "Cool Optic II." (Taylor)

RF-101G/H

As mentioned earlier, twenty-nine F-101As were converted to RF-101Gs and thirty-two F-101Cs were converted to RF-101Hs as the fighter versions were withdrawn from service. Reports also indicate that at least two RF-101As were included in the RF-101G numbers. These conversions produced aircraft capable of daylight low-level reconnaissance, and the aircraft were assigned directly into Air National Guard units of Kentucky, Arkansas, and Nevada. First delivery of the aircraft to the squadrons was in 1966.

Among several deployments flown by these units, the most notable was an activation to provide reconnaissance during the Pueblo crisis in early 1968. Each of the three units rotated in turn to Itazuke AB, Japan, in order to carry out this mission. Other deployments included three months in the Canal Zone and five months to Elmendorf AFB, Alaska, by Kentucky's 123rd TRW.

Head-on view of an RF-101H showing the modified camera nose. (Taylor)

25

The nose of the RF-101G/H slid forward for access. This photo shows a Kentucky ANG aircraft being serviced during "Cool Optic II." (Taylor)

Underside view showing the camera installations under the nose of an RF-101H. Also note the two blade antennas behind the row of camera windows.

Another view of the camera windows. This photo shows the shape of the forward camera fairing to good effect.

This close-up shows how the gun ports of the F-101As and -Cs were closed over during the conversion to a camera laden nose.

The Nevada ANG flew F-101Bs that were converted to RF-101Bs. As was the case with the RF-101G/H, the RF-101B conversion was an attempt to maintain the number of tactical reconnaissance assets in the Air Force at acceptable, but rather minimal, levels. Tactical reconnaissance aircraft, like the RF-101s and RF-4s suffered significant losses in SEA.
(Taylor)

RF-101B

Due to further losses of RF-101Cs in Vietnam, an F-101B was converted to an RF-101B test aircraft. After proving successful, twenty-two of Canada's first batch of CF-101Bs (returned to the U.S. for a second batch) were converted to RF-101Bs and assigned to the Nevada ANG (192nd TRS) beginning in late 1971 and early 1972. Nevada sent its RF-101Hs to Kentucky, and Kentucky sent its -Gs to Arkansas, so that each unit then operated only one type of aircraft.

Left side of the nose of an RF-101B in flight.
(McDonnell Douglas)

Close-up of the camera nose on an RF-101B.
(Taylor)

F-101 DIMENSIONS

DIMENSION	ACTUAL	1/72	1/48	1/32
Length (F-101A/C)	67.4 ft	11.24 in	16.85 in	25.28 in
Length (RF-101A/C)	69.3 ft	11.55 in	17.33 in	25.99 in
Length (F-101B)	71.1 ft	11.85 in	17.78 in	26.66 in
Wingspan	39.7 ft	6.62 in	9.93 in	14.89 in
Height	18.0 ft	3.00 in	4.50 in	6.75 in
Tread	19.9 ft	3.32 in	4.98 in	7.45 in

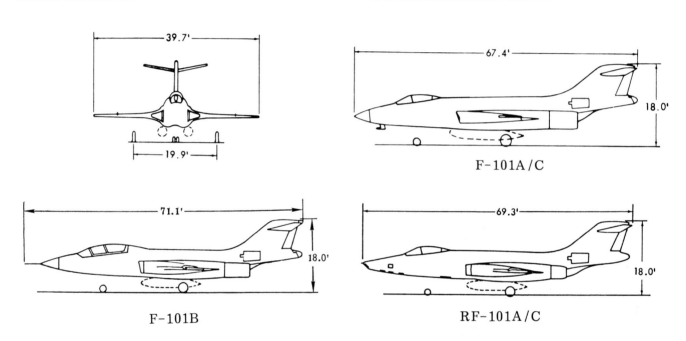

F-101A/C

F-101B

RF-101A/C

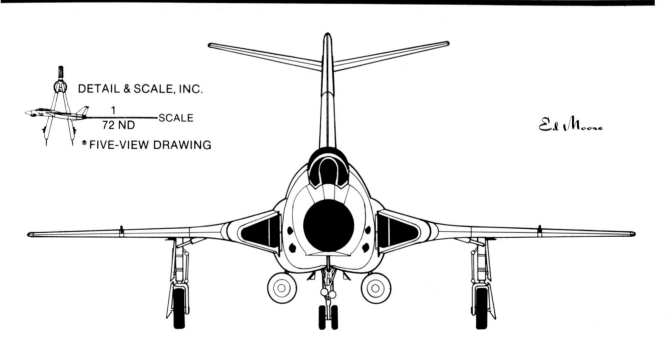

DETAIL & SCALE, INC.

$\frac{1}{72 \text{ ND}}$ ——SCALE

® FIVE-VIEW DRAWING

Ed Moore

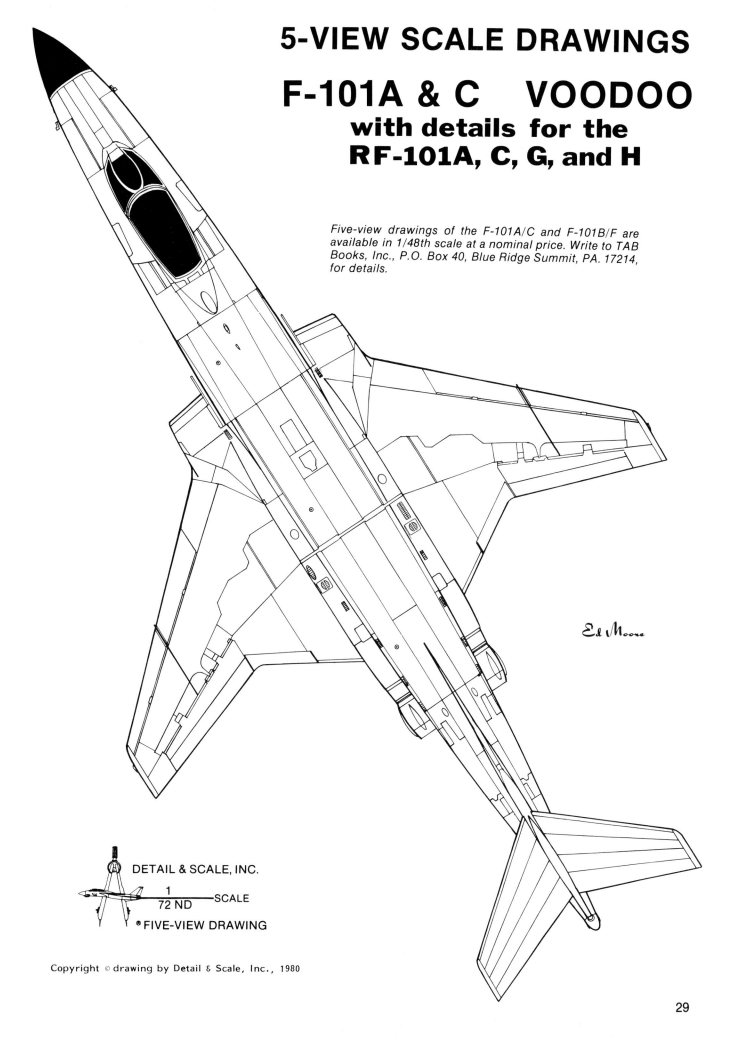

5-VIEW SCALE DRAWINGS

F-101A & C   VOODOO
with details for the RF-101A, C, G, and H

Five-view drawings of the F-101A/C and F-101B/F are available in 1/48th scale at a nominal price. Write to TAB Books, Inc., P.O. Box 40, Blue Ridge Summit, PA. 17214, for details.

Ed Moore

DETAIL & SCALE, INC.

$$\frac{1}{72\ ND}$$ SCALE

® FIVE-VIEW DRAWING

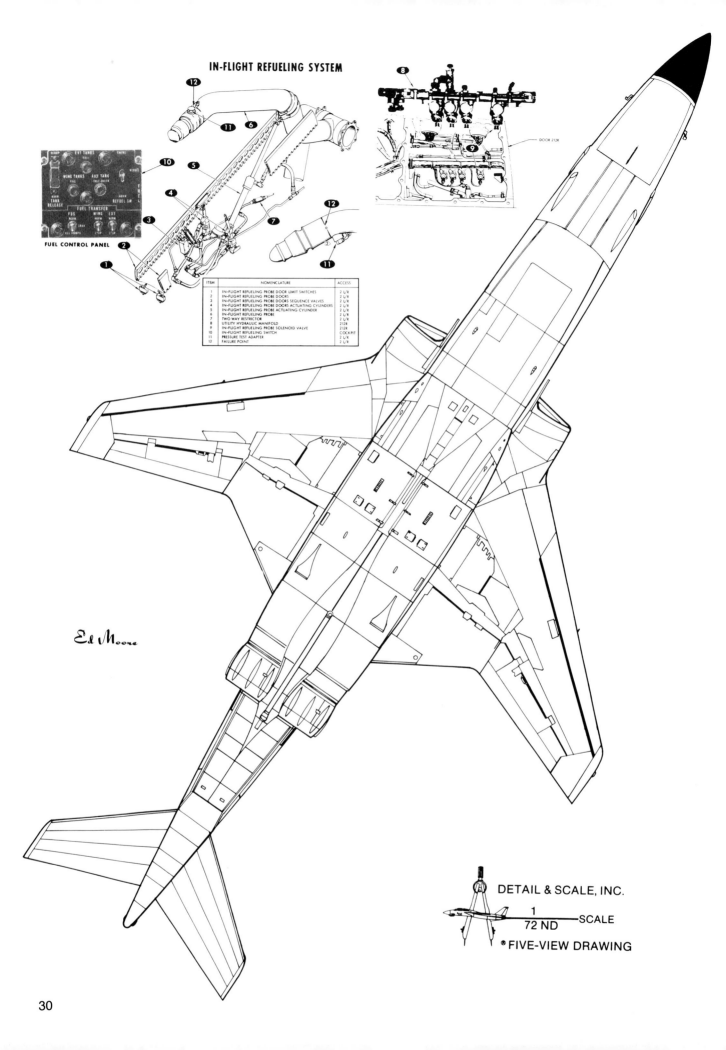

IN-FLIGHT REFUELING SYSTEM

FUEL CONTROL PANEL

ITEM	NOMENCLATURE	ACCESS
1	IN-FLIGHT REFUELING PROBE DOOR LIMIT SWITCHES	2 L/R
2	IN-FLIGHT REFUELING PROBE DOORS	2 L/R
3	IN-FLIGHT REFUELING PROBE DOORS SEQUENCE VALVES	2 L/R
4	IN-FLIGHT REFUELING PROBE DOORS ACTUATING CYLINDERS	2 L/R
5	IN-FLIGHT REFUELING PROBE ACTUATING CYLINDER	2 L/R
6	IN-FLIGHT REFUELING PROBE	2 L/R
7	TWO WAY RESTRICTOR	2 L/R
8	UTILITY HYDRAULIC MANIFOLD	212R
9	IN-FLIGHT REFUELING PROBE SOLENOID VALVE	212R
10	IN-FLIGHT REFUELING SWITCH	COCKPIT
11	PRESSURE TEST ADAPTER	2 L/R
12	FAILURE POINT	2 L/R

Ed Moore

DETAIL & SCALE, INC.

SCALE 1/72 ND

® FIVE-VIEW DRAWING

CAMOUFLAGE SCHEME

Detail drawings courtesy
of the U.S. Air Force.

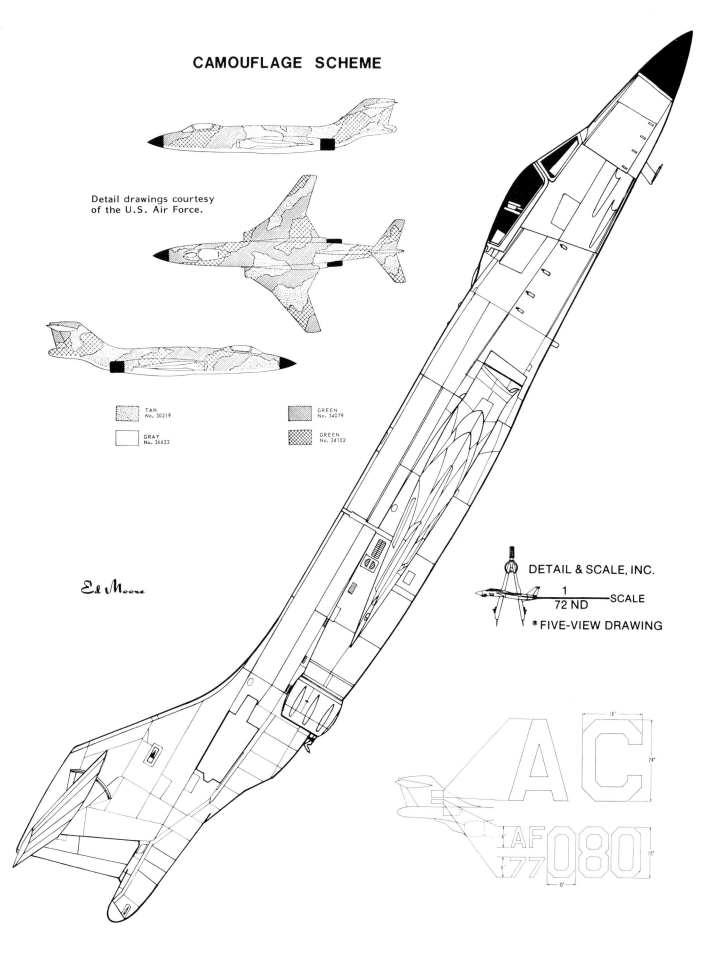

Ed Moore

| | TAN No. 30219 | | GREEN No. 34079 |
| | GRAY No. 36622 | | GREEN No. 34102 |

DETAIL & SCALE, INC.

$\frac{1}{72\ ND}$ SCALE

® FIVE-VIEW DRAWING

AC

AF 77 080

18"

24"

6"

15"

10"

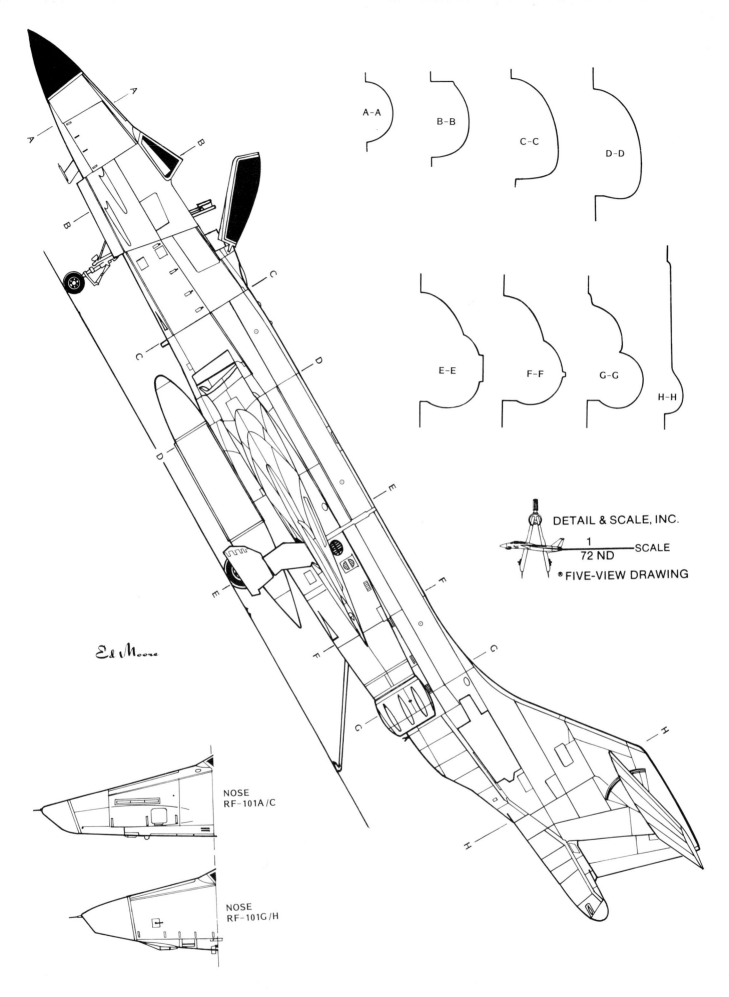

A-A

B-B

C-C

D-D

E-E

F-F

G-G

H-H

DETAIL & SCALE, INC.

$\dfrac{1}{72\ ND}$ ——— SCALE

® FIVE-VIEW DRAWING

Ed Moore

NOSE
RF-101A/C

NOSE
RF-101G/H

F-101A/C COLORS

A highly polished F-101A-5-MC, 53-2426, is seen at Edwards AFB during flight testing. High visibility orange is painted under the nose, wing, and tail areas. The radome and some panels on the nose have been painted gray. This aircraft was named "Fire Wall," and was used to set an absolute world speed record of 1207 MPH on December 12, 1957. Careful examination of this photograph will reveal the larger afterburner cans used on the F-101B. These were used during the setting of the speed record.

(Baker via Leader)

F-101A-35-MC, 54-1475, of the 81st TFW as photographed on March 31, 1966, at Shaw AFB, S.C.. Note the bright silver paint around the engines and on the upper portions of the center fuselage section.

(Taylor)

F-101As of the 92nd TFS, 81st TFW seen in Spain in 1961. The tails, wing tips, and wing fences are yellow.

(Snyder via Taylor)

A former F-101C, converted to an RF-101H, is shown during an approach to landing. Along with their guns, the former "fighting 101s" also gave up their more colorful paint schemes. Notice the extension of the landing gear struts in flight.

(Picciani)

RF-101C COLORS

Above: RF-101A-30-MC, 54-1515, as it appeared in May 1957. This was General Mack's personal aircraft while he was commander of the 9th Air Force. (Taylor collection)

Left: This RF-101C is shown in the colors of the 363rd TRW. The 363rd included the 20th TRS, 29th TRS, and 4414th CCTS. (Picciani)

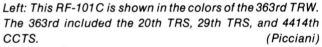

These two photos show the end of the RF-101C. The aircraft were from the Mississippi ANG, and, when photographed in January 1979 in El Paso, Texas, they were on their way to the "boneyard" at Davis Monthan AFB. Four aircraft took off together, making the last formation flight by RF-101Cs, and 56-081, shown at right, took off later, being the last RF-101C to fly.

RF-101C COCKPIT COLORS

Above: Instrument panel detail in an RF-101C.

Right: Area behind the seat showing canopy raising and lowering mechanism.

Below: Left and right consoles in an RF-101C.

F-101B COCKPIT COLORS

Visible in this photo is the area above the main instrument panel in the front cockpit of an F-101B. The combining glass and magnetic compass are visible.

Front instrument panel in an F-101B.

Center panel between the rudder pedals in the front cockpit.

Control column detail.

Left console showing throttles.

Right console detail. The oxygen hose and microphone lines rest on the seat.

Rear instrument panel in an F-101B.

Radar scope in the rear cockpit without the hood attached.

Radar scope with hood attached. The hood is usually stowed in a mount located on the aft end of the canopy.

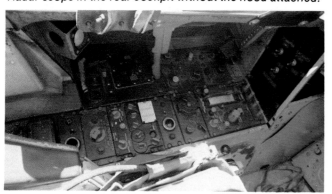

F-101B left rear console.

Right rear console showing the radar observer's antenna hand control grip.

Compare these photos to those of the F-101F rear cockpit shown on page 50.

MG-13 FIRE CONTROL SYSTEM

The Hughes MG-13 fire control system filled the entire nose of the F-101B forward of the windscreen and nose gear well. Above is the system as viewed from the left side, while at right is a front view of the radar dish antenna.

At right is a view of the radar and its mounting equipment as viewed from the right, while the photo above shows the left side view of the radar and its mount.

Right and left side bays showing MG-13 equipment. Today, solid state technology would reduce the size and weight of this system to a fraction of what it was in the F-101B. Maintainability would also be improved.

F-101B COLORS

This interesting photo shows an early F-101B on display at an air show. The sign on the nose of the aircraft indicates that the aircraft is an RF-101A, and the slide from which this photo was made is marked as such. In the background is a B-47.

(Jones)

At left is a Texas ANG F-101B, photographed on October 18, 1980. The Oregon ANG is represented by F-101B-110-MC, 58-0312, shown at right.

(Both Flightleader)

North Dakota's "Happy Hooligans" flew F-101Bs until giving them up for F-4Ds. At right is an aircraft from the Maine "Bangors" at the 1972 William Tell Weapons Meet.

(Left Flightleader, right Munkasy)

Taken on September 5, 1973, this photo shows F-101B-100-MC, 57-0423, in the markings of the Minnesota ANG.

These two photos show Canadian CF-101Bs in standard markings. At left is an aircraft from the 409 "Night Hawk" Squadron. It is painted silver overall. The aircraft at right is painted overall gray, and is from the 416 "Black Lynx" Squadron. The photo is dated May 5, 1978, while the one at left was taken in July 1974. (Left Swanberg via Leader, right Flightleader)

Two unusual and very colorful schemes worn by Canadian CF-101Bs are shown in these photos. At left is "Hawk One Canada," belonging to the 409 "Night Hawk" Squadron as photographed in September 1977. The photo at right shows "Alouette Un Canada," of the 425th AW(F) "Alouette" Squadron. "Lark One Canada" was painted on the opposite side of the fuselage.
(Left Swanberg via Leader, right Soulaine)

F-101B

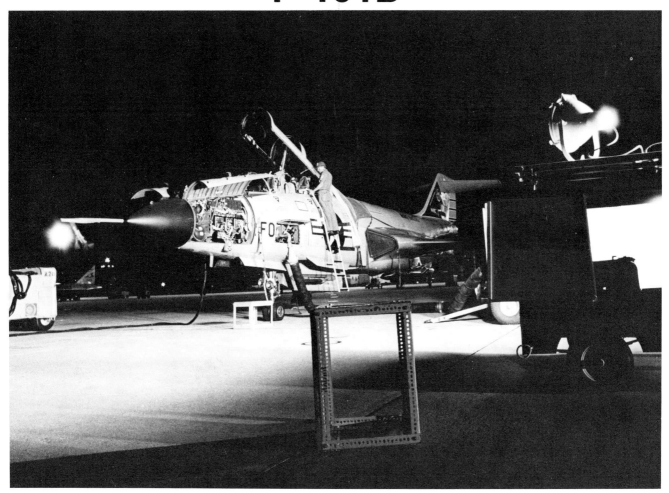

A Maine ANG F-101B receives some maintenance man hours in the cool Bangor night air.   (USAF via Barbier)

Easily the most successful and best known version of the Voodoo was the F-101B interceptor. A total of 480 two-seaters were built, and served the U.S. Air Force's active interceptor squadrons, the Air National Guard, and the Canadian Air Force for many years.

The F-101B was McDonnell's Model 36 AT, Weapon System 217A, and differed from the F-101A/C in a number of ways. Most noticeable was the second cockpit, located behind the first, resulting in a reduction of fuselage fuel capacity. Some sources report that the fuselage was lengthened to accommodate the second cockpit, but this was not the case. The longer length given for the F-101B (as compared to the F-101A/C) includes a long pitot static boom that was mounted on the nose. This was not present on the F-101A/C.

Other new features included longer afterburner cans on the J57-P-55 engines, upgraded from the -13 engines on the other models. The four 20mm cannon were replaced with a rotary weapons bay with two AIM-4 Falcon IR guided missiles, and two nuclear AIR-2A Genie rockets. The Hughes MG-13 radar fire control system was placed in the nose. At one point, three Falcons and 2.75 inch rockets were to arm the F-101B, as they were the F-101A/C, but this was changed before production began.

The rotary weapons bay and missiles were first flight tested on a specially modified F-101A. This is where it was learned that strakes were needed on either side of the weapons bay door to protect the intakes from air turbulance caused by the AIR-2 Genies.   (McDonnell Douglas via Taylor)

This cut-away shows the early configuration planned for the F-101B. Originally, the -B was to carry three AIM-4 Falcons and rockets in the weapons bay door. This may explain why some publications still state that the F-101B carried three Falcons. Actually, the production aircraft carried only two Falcons and no rockets, except for the large, nuclear capable AIR-2 Genies.
(McDonnell Douglas)

Another difference involved the main landing gear, and was necessitated by the interceptor version's greater weight. Larger tires were used with a beefed-up gear, and bulges in the lower gear doors and undersides of the fuselage were added to accept the width of the larger tires. (See pages 12 and 13.)

The Air Force designated the interceptor version of the Voodoo the F-101B in August 1955, and the mock-up inspection was held the following month. The first flight was made on March 27, 1957, from Lambert Field. Extensive flight testing continued for almost two years before the F-101B entered operational service with the 60th FIS at Otis AFB in January 1959. Shortly, seventeen of ADCs Fighter Interceptor Squadrons were equipped with the F-101B.

Like other versions of the Voodoo, the F-101B suffered

In July 1972, this former 60th FIS F-101B had been transferred to the New York ANG, and is shown at Niagara Falls in New York's early markings. (Geer)

from corrosion and skin cracks. Originally delivered in overall bare metal, they were later painted silver to help prevent corrosion. This was later changed to overall ADC gray, and most remained in this gray throughout their service life.

McDonnell provided dual-control kits to be placed in the rear cockpit for instructional purposes. At least fifty were built and fitted in F-101Bs, changing their designations to TF-101Bs. Later, McDonnell began producing dual-control aircraft on the assembly line, and these were designated F-101Fs. Only limited flight controls were provided in the rear cockpit, and there were no external differences between the -B and -F. On February 3, 1961, all dual-control aircraft were designated F-101F.

Although the F-101B did not set any world speed records like the F-101A/C and RF-101C, it did fly the first supersonic interception on June 9, 1958. It was also the first interceptor to have in-flight refueling capability. Originally, both in-flight refueling systems were available. Later, when the IR sensor and fairing was added to the nose, the probe and drogue system was deleted.

Except for a few RF-101As provided to Nationalist China, Canada was the only foreign country to operate the Voodoo. In October 1961, Canada received the first of sixty-six interceptors to include ten TF-101B dual-control versions. The Canadian aircraft were designated CF-101Bs and CF-101Fs, the later designation being for the dual-control aircraft.

Although the RCAF has retired its Voodoo interceptors from service, two aircraft remain with Number 414 Squadron at North Bay. At left is 101067 in its overall black finish with red markings. It is being used as an electronic countermeasures aircraft. At right is 101006 which is overall gray. It was one of the second batch of Voodoos received by Canada. These two aircraft are the last of any type of F-101 to fly, and are scheduled to be phased out of service in 1986. (Soulaine)

Canada obtained its Voodoos in return for manning NORAD radar sites, also vital in the air defense of the North American continent. Five Canadian squadrons (409th "Night Hawk," 410th "Cougar," 414th "Black Knight," 416th "Lynx" and 425th "Alouette") received the Voodoos. Originally the Canadian aircraft were not capable of firing the nuclear Genie, but the nuclear capability was added later.

Beginning in 1969, and extending through 1971, "Operation Peace Wings" provided Canada with sixty-six updated F-101Bs, and Canada returned the fifty-six remaining aircraft of the initial batch. Again, ten dual-control -Fs were included. The easy way to tell a Canadian Voodoo of the first batch from one of the second batch is to look for the IR sensor on the nose. If present, the aircraft is from the second batch. If not, it is from the first batch.

The Canadian Voodoos of the second batch also had many other improvements not found on their first aircraft. These included modifications that had been added to Air Force F-101B/Fs on an almost continuing basis. Beginning in 1963, the Interceptor Improvement Program (IIP) increased the aircraft's capability to intercept airbreathing missiles and aircraft, and reduced its vulnerability to electronic countermeasures. The radar was improved to detect and track low flying targets. Other changes were initiated as fixes to various problems. Separate pneumatic starters

were provided for each engine. Early starters had proved unreliable, and had resulted in a number of injuries to ground personnel. An improved pitch control system was installed in an effort to lessen the ever present pitch-up problem.

As the F-101B was phased out of the active inventory, Air National Guard squadrons began receiving the aircraft in 1969, replacing F-102 Delta Daggers. Air National Guard units from Oregon, New York, Minnesota, Texas, North Dakota, Maine, and Washington all flew the F-101B/F. Finally, on August 8, 1983, a Texas ANG F-101F made the last flight of a Guard Voodoo, leaving only the Canadian aircraft to follow it out of service a short time later.

As of this writing, two Voodoos remain in service with the RCAF's Number 414 Squadron based at North Bay. CF-101F, 101006, is a leftover from the second batch of Voodoos received under Operation Peace Wings. It is being used in a training role. The second aircraft is an unusual Voodoo in a unique overall gloss black scheme. Designated EC-101B, and numbered 101067, this aircraft was obtained from the U.S. Air Force as a special acquisition, separate from the two batches of Voodoos previously received by Canada. It is used as an electronic countermeasures aircraft. These two aircraft are expected to remain in use through 1986, and will become the last F-101s of any type to be retired.

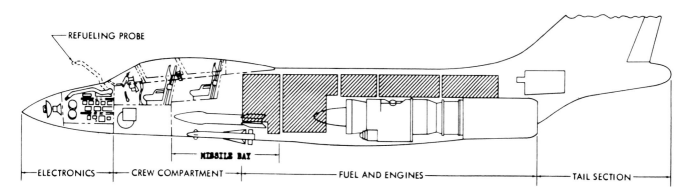

REFUELING PROBE

MISSILE BAY

ELECTRONICS — CREW COMPARTMENT — FUEL AND ENGINES — TAIL SECTION

F-101B/F 5-VIEW SCALE DRAWINGS

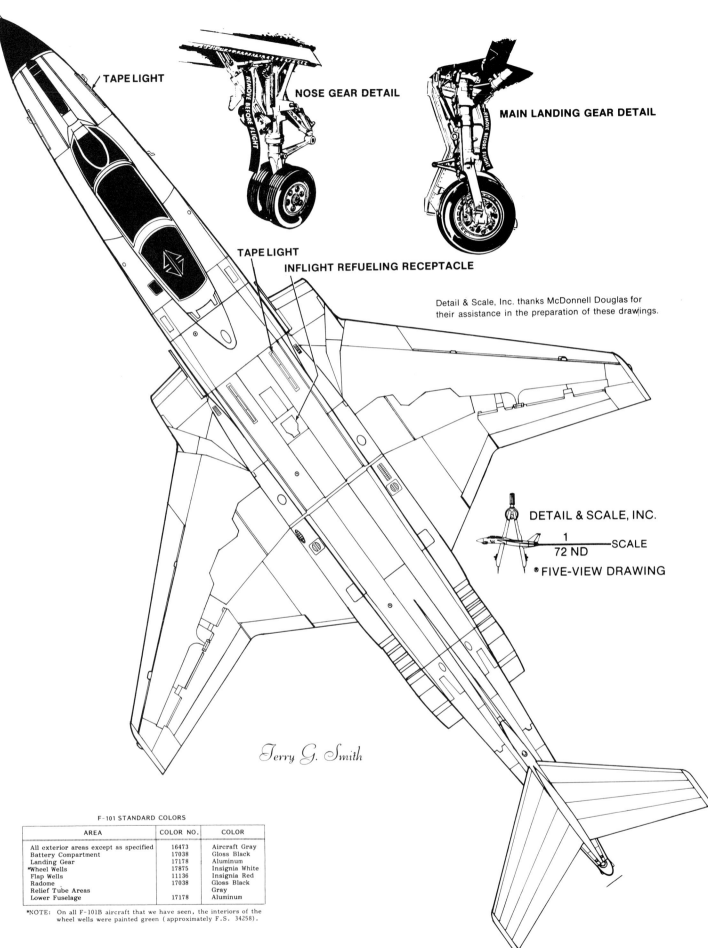

TAPE LIGHT

NOSE GEAR DETAIL

MAIN LANDING GEAR DETAIL

TAPE LIGHT

INFLIGHT REFUELING RECEPTACLE

Detail & Scale, Inc. thanks McDonnell Douglas for their assistance in the preparation of these drawings.

DETAIL & SCALE, INC.

$$\frac{1}{72\,ND}$$ SCALE

® FIVE-VIEW DRAWING

Jerry G. Smith

F-101 STANDARD COLORS

AREA	COLOR NO.	COLOR
All exterior areas except as specified	16473	Aircraft Gray
Battery Compartment	17038	Gloss Black
Landing Gear	17178	Aluminum
*Wheel Wells	17875	Insignia White
Flap Wells	11136	Insignia Red
Radome	17038	Gloss Black
Relief Tube Areas		Gray
Lower Fuselage	17178	Aluminum

*NOTE: On all F-101B aircraft that we have seen, the interiors of the wheel wells were painted green (approximately F.S. 34258).

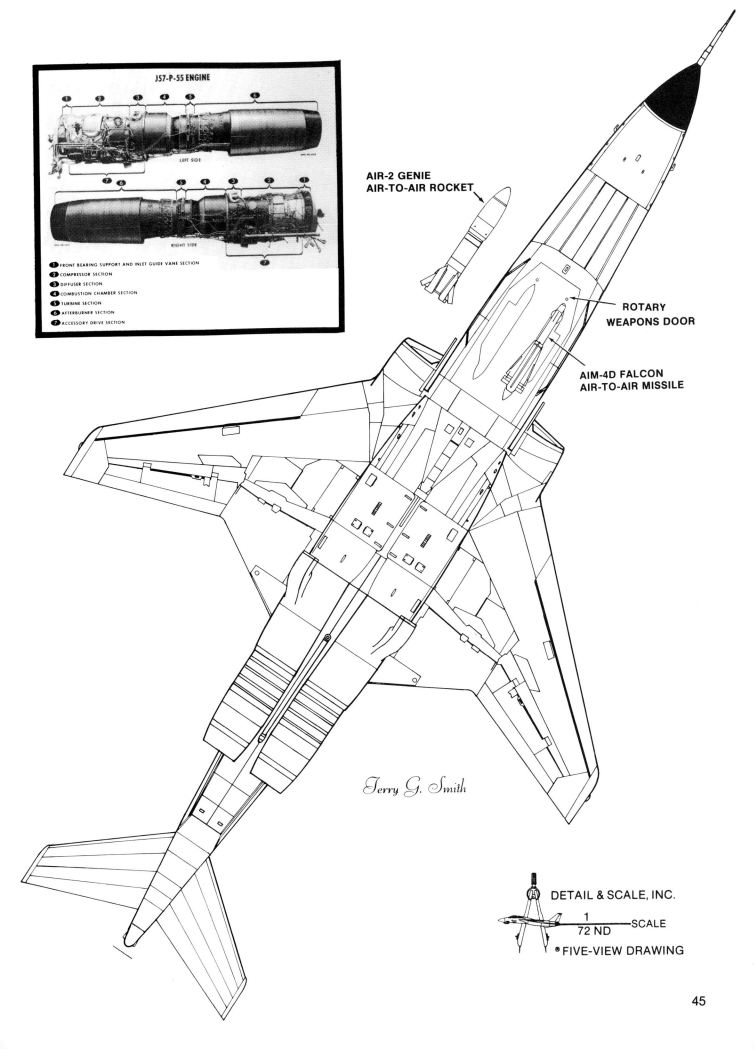

J57-P-55 ENGINE

LEFT SIDE

RIGHT SIDE

1. FRONT BEARING SUPPORT AND INLET GUIDE VANE SECTION
2. COMPRESSOR SECTION
3. DIFFUSER SECTION
4. COMBUSTION CHAMBER SECTION
5. TURBINE SECTION
6. AFTERBURNER SECTION
7. ACCESSORY DRIVE SECTION

AIR-2 GENIE
AIR-TO-AIR ROCKET

ROTARY
WEAPONS DOOR

AIM-4D FALCON
AIR-TO-AIR MISSILE

Jerry G. Smith

DETAIL & SCALE, INC.

$\frac{1}{72 \text{ ND}}$ ——SCALE

® FIVE-VIEW DRAWING

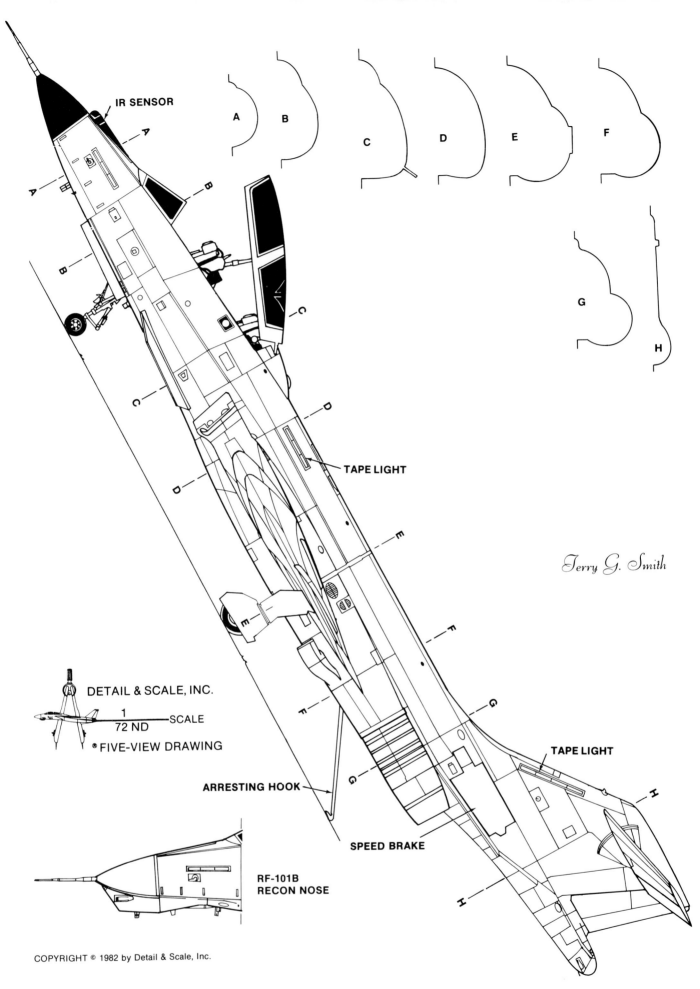

IR SENSOR

A

B

C

D

E

F

G

H

TAPE LIGHT

TAPE LIGHT

Jerry G. Smith

DETAIL & SCALE, INC.

$\dfrac{1}{72\ ND}$ ⎯ SCALE

® FIVE-VIEW DRAWING

ARRESTING HOOK

SPEED BRAKE

RF-101B
RECON NOSE

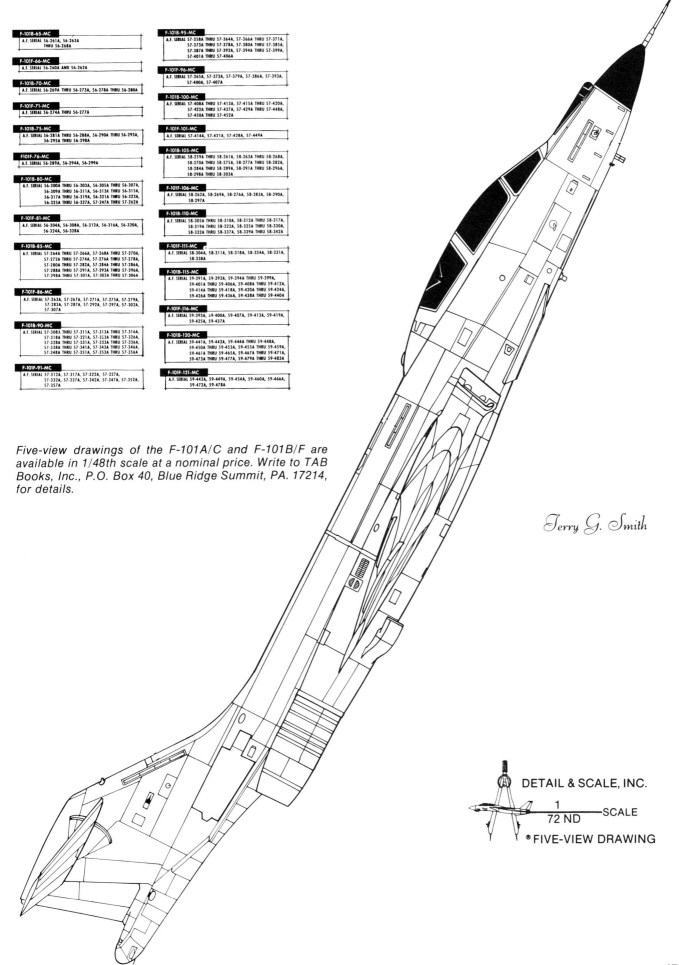

F-101B-65-MC
A.F. SERIAL 56-261A, 56-263A THRU 56-268A

F-101F-66-MC
A.F. SERIAL 56-260A AND 56-262A

F-101B-70-MC
A.F. SERIAL 56-269A THRU 56-273A, 56-278A THRU 56-280A

F-101F-71-MC
A.F. SERIAL 56-274A THRU 56-277A

F-101B-75-MC
A.F. SERIAL 56-281A THRU 56-288A, 56-290A THRU 56-293A, 56-295A THRU 56-298A

F101F-76-MC
A.F. SERIAL 56-289A, 56-294A, 56-299A

F-101B-80-MC
A.F. SERIAL 56-300A THRU 56-303A, 56-305A THRU 56-307A, 56-309A THRU 56-311A, 56-313A THRU 56-315A, 56-317A THRU 56-319A, 56-321A THRU 56-323A, 56-325A THRU 56-327A, 57-247A THRU 57-262A

F-101F-81-MC
A.F. SERIAL 56-304A, 56-308A, 56-312A, 56-316A, 56-320A, 56-324A, 56-328A

F-101B-85-MC
A.F. SERIAL 57-264A THRU 57-266A, 57-268A THRU 57-270A, 57-272A THRU 57-274A, 57-276A THRU 57-278A, 57-280A THRU 57-282A, 57-284A THRU 57-286A, 57-288A THRU 57-291A, 57-293A THRU 57-296A, 57-298A THRU 57-301A, 57-303A THRU 57-306A

F-101F-86-MC
A.F. SERIAL 57-263A, 57-267A, 57-271A, 57-275A, 57-279A, 57-283A, 57-287A, 57-292A, 57-297A, 57-302A, 57-307A

F-101B-90-MC
A.F. SERIAL 57-308A THRU 57-311A, 57-313A THRU 57-316A, 57-318A THRU 57-321A, 57-323A THRU 57-326A, 57-328A THRU 57-331A, 57-333A THRU 57-336A, 57-338A THRU 57-341A, 57-343A THRU 57-346A, 57-348A THRU 57-351A, 57-353A THRU 57-356A

F-101F-91-MC
A.F. SERIAL 57-312A, 57-317A, 57-322A, 57-327A, 57-332A, 57-337A, 57-342A, 57-347A, 57-352A, 57-357A

F-101B-95-MC
A.F. SERIAL 57-358A THRU 57-364A, 57-366A THRU 57-371A, 57-373A THRU 57-378A, 57-380A THRU 57-385A, 57-387A THRU 57-392A, 57-394A THRU 57-399A, 57-401A THRU 57-406A

F-101F-96-MC
A.F. SERIAL 57-365A, 57-372A, 57-379A, 57-386A, 57-393A, 57-400A, 57-407A

F-101B-100-MC
A.F. SERIAL 57-408A THRU 57-413A, 57-415A THRU 57-420A, 57-422A THRU 57-427A, 57-429A THRU 57-448A, 57-450A THRU 57-452A

F-101F-101-MC
A.F. SERIAL 57-414A, 57-421A, 57-428A, 57-449A

F-101B-105-MC
A.F. SERIAL 58-259A THRU 58-261A, 58-263A THRU 58-268A, 58-270A THRU 58-275A, 58-277A THRU 58-282A, 58-284A THRU 58-289A, 58-291A THRU 58-296A, 58-298A THRU 58-303A

F-101F-106-MC
A.F. SERIAL 58-262A, 58-269A, 58-276A, 58-283A, 58-290A, 58-297A

F-101B-110-MC
A.F. SERIAL 58-305A THRU 58-310A, 58-312A THRU 58-317A, 58-319A THRU 58-323A, 58-325A THRU 58-330A, 58-332A THRU 58-337A, 58-339A THRU 58-342A

F-101F-111-MC
A.F. SERIAL 58-304A, 58-311A, 58-318A, 58-324A, 58-331A, 58-338A

F-101B-115-MC
A.F. SERIAL 59-391A, 59-392A, 59-394A THRU 59-399A, 59-401A THRU 59-406A, 59-408A THRU 59-412A, 59-414A THRU 59-418A, 59-420A THRU 59-424A, 59-426A THRU 59-436A, 59-438A THRU 59-440A

F-101F-116-MC
A.F. SERIAL 59-393A, 59-400A, 59-407A, 59-413A, 59-419A, 59-425A, 59-437A

F-101B-120-MC
A.F. SERIAL 59-442A, 59-444A THRU 59-448A, 59-450A THRU 59-453A, 59-455A THRU 59-459A, 59-461A THRU 59-465A, 59-467A THRU 59-471A, 59-473A THRU 59-477A, 59-479A THRU 59-483A

F-101F-121-MC
A.F. SERIAL 59-443A, 59-449A, 59-454A, 59-460A, 59-466A, 59-472A, 59-478A

Five-view drawings of the F-101A/C and F-101B/F are available in 1/48th scale at a nominal price. Write to TAB Books, Inc., P.O. Box 40, Blue Ridge Summit, PA. 17214, for details.

Terry G. Smith

DETAIL & SCALE, INC.

$\dfrac{1}{72\text{ ND}}$ SCALE

® FIVE-VIEW DRAWING

47

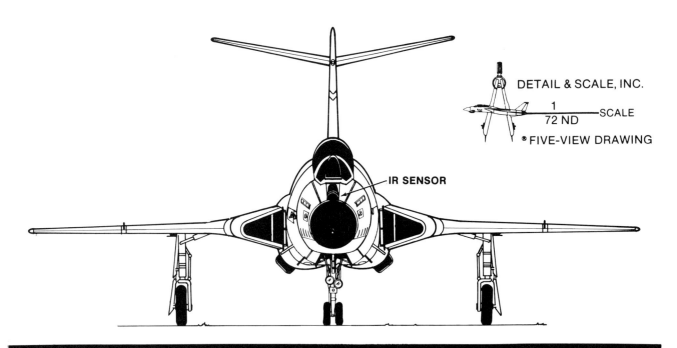

DETAIL & SCALE, INC.

$\dfrac{1}{72\text{ ND}}$ SCALE

® FIVE-VIEW DRAWING

IR SENSOR

Front instrument panel in a Canadian CF-101B. Compare this photo to the F-101B panel shown on page 36, and the F-101F front panel shown on the next page.

(Dielwart via Barbier)

F-101F COCKPIT DETAIL

FRONT COCKPIT

The front cockpit in the F-101F is practically the same as that in the F-101B. In this photo a hood has been added over the radar scope, and the control column has been removed, revealing the center panel.

Left auxiliary panel.

Right auxiliary panel.

Left console detail.

Right front console.

Above: The dual-control F-101F had basic flight controls in the rear cockpit. This included a control column, not present in the rear cockpit of an F-101B.

Above right: A Plexiglas shield protected the rear seat crewmember in the event the canopy was lost. This was on both the F-101B and F-101F.

Rear instrument panel detail in an F-101F.

The left rear console in an F-101F included throttles, not present in the F-101B.

The right rear console in the F-101F was essentially the same as that in the F-101B, and included the radar control handle.

F-101B/F DETAILS

NOSE DETAILS

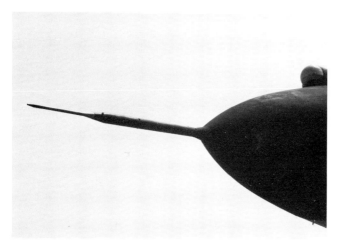

Close-up of the pitot static boom.

Underside of nose showing AN/ARN-21 TACAN and AN/ARN-32 Marker Beacon antenna panels. The blade antenna is the lower UHF antenna.

Upper nose area showing the IR seeker and fairing which was retrofitted to F-101B/Fs over the doors that originally covered the refueling probe. The formation light panels were also added. The luminescent portion of the nose panels is 34½ inches long, divided into three equal segments. The panels are two inches high, and the gaps between the panel segments are ¼ inch in size.

Three hot air exhaust vent holes are located just to the left of the aft end of the nose gear well, and just forward of the rotary weapons bay door.

On early F-101Bs, a primary refrigeration air intake slot was located just to the left of the nose gear, as seen in the photo at left. This was later replaced with the scoop shown at right. However, Canadian Voodoos retained the slot throughout their service life.

The angle of attack transmitter is located between the U. and S. on the right side of the nose.

At the William Tell Weapons meet in 1972, this ADWC F-101B had an unusual fairing under the nose. The small insignia on the fairing is that of the Army's Hawk Air Defense Missile System.

Right and left side close-up views of the nose show the two alpha probes which provide pressure data on altitude and airspeed, as well as angle of attack information. They are part of the MB-5 Automatic Pilot System.

The small blade antenna, located next to the right nose gear door, was the IFF antenna before the incorporation of T.O. 1F-101-1197, and the transponder antenna afterward. Both serve an identification function. At right is the total temperature probe.

CANOPY DETAILS

Windscreen as viewed from the front. The combining glass is visible through the center section.

This view shows the fairing behind the canopy, and the canopy hinge. A transponder blade antenna, upper fuselage white light, and a red beacon light are located on this fairing.

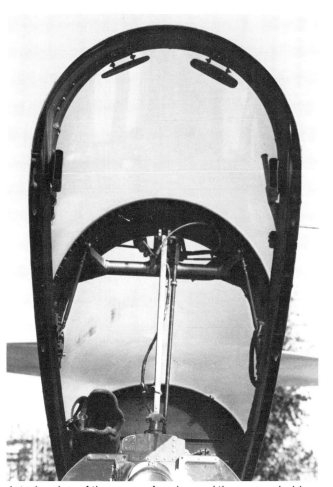

Interior view of the canopy framing and the canopy hold-up brace.

These two views show the single canopy covering both cockpits. Some framing details are also visible.

At left is a photo of the back of the canopy with the hood for the rear cockpit radar scope in its stowed position. At right is the area behind the rear seat. Note the hydraulic piston used for raising and lowering the canopy.

ROTARY WEAPONS BAY DOOR

Rotary weapons bay door rotated 90 degrees showing the side used to carry the AIR-2 Genie rockets.

View looking aft at the Genie side of the bay door.

Above: AIM-4D Falcon missiles were carried on this side of the weapons bay door.

Left: Several vanes were placed ahead of the left Falcon well in order to deflect hot air that was being discharged from the three vents shown ahead of the door. The hot air was affecting the IR seeker head of the missile.

Genie side of the armament door looking forward.

ARMAMENT

Above: Falcons shown in place under a Canadian CF-101B.

Above right: Falcon training simulator missile in place on the weapons bay door with the door rotated 90 degrees.

Right: AIR-2 Genies in place on the armament door.

Armament was not all that was carried on the rotary door. These two photos show a travel pod attached to the AIR-2 side. A spare engine starter is attached to the front of the pod.

FUSELAGE DETAILS

General view of the left side of the fuselage forward of the air intake. The shape of the strake is clearly visible in this view.

Close-up of details on the forward left fuselage, just above the strake. The two dark circles in the national insignia (one in the star and one in the blue surround) are actually glass viewing holes to check the primary hydraulic reservoir and the pressure gage. The lighter circle, at the bottom of the national insignia, is a ground point. Just below and to the right is the lower fuselage light.

The right side of the forward fuselage has small circular glass windows to check the utility hydraulic reservoir and accumulator. The right side lower fuselage light is also visible in this photo.

Close-up of the large ID light located on the left side of the fuselage, even with the rear cockpit's ejection seat. The light served an identification function at night.

This photo shows the fuselage formation light panel on the left side. It has three segments, and is thirty-seven inches long.

View of the strake on the right side. The proper name for the strakes on either side of the weapons bay door is "aerodynamic flow fence."

A drain strut is located under each engine, and exits the fuselage through the engine fairing. It is part of the engine fuel pump, and its purpose is to drain out any fuel from the system when the engine is shut down.

F-101Bs were retrofitted with flat spring type arrestor hooks for emergency barrier landings. The hook was located between the engines and afterburners as shown.

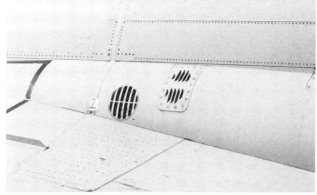

Bleed air vents are located on each side on the fuselage on the engine fairings, just above the wing. Those shown in the photo at left are on the right side of the fuselage, and those in the right photo are on the left side. Note that the forward vents on each side are different in shape. However, they both are for the compressor bleed system for each engine.

Secondary air scoops replaced flush intake slots on the F-101B/F, and provided cooling for the aft engine bays. Intake slots remained on other versions of the Voodoo.

This in-flight view shows the larger afterburner cans of the F-101B/F to good effect. Also note the data link antennas and the open speed brakes. *(Dielwart via Barbier)*

At left is a view looking into the left afterburner can showing the variable nozzle vanes. At right is a close-up of the left afterburner can with the protective cover in place. The stick with alternating dark and light segments is a ruler marked off in inches.

Close-up detail of the data link antennas which are located under the right engine.

Belly fuselage light located on the centerline between the external fuel tank connections.

FUEL TANKS & CONNECTIONS

All F-101s could carry two 450 gallon drop tanks that were attached directly to the fuselage. There were two styles of tanks. The ones most often seen were the shorter ones with a larger diameter as seen in this photo. The other style was longer with a smaller diameter, offering less drag and greater speed.

Fuel tank connections on the right side with the tank in place.

Fuel tank connections on the left side looking aft.

Above each external tank is an access panel that opens for inspection of primary and utility hydraulic recepticles for the tanks.

INTAKES & ENGINE BAYS

Voodoos had an intake for each engine mounted in the wing roots. These intakes were of relatively simple design with a fixed ramp and a splitter plate inside the opening. At left is the right intake on an F-101B with the ever-present walkway painted on top of it. At right is a view looking down on the top of the left intake showing the braces between the fixed ramp and the fuselage.

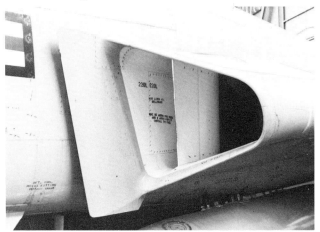

Left intake from the front showing the fixed ramp and splitter plate inside the intake to good effect.

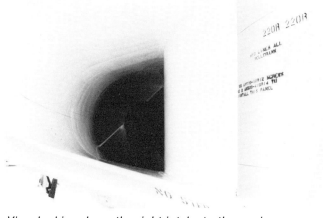

View looking down the right intake to the engine.

These two photos were taken looking forward in the two engine bays with the engines removed. The insides of the intakes can be seen at the end of each bay, and the cooling scoops are visible in the foreground of each picture.

OPEN
ACCESS PANELS

Above: Primary access panels are shown open on the right side of the aircraft. The forward panel on both sides provided access to the MG-13 Fire Control System.

Above right: Door 207R covered various electrical equipment.

Right: Panels 212R and 213R are shown open revealing details of the utility hydraulic system (forward), and the right side of the missile auxiliaries bay.

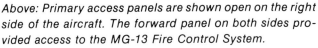

At left is panel 207L, which is opened to reveal the refrigeration unit and ground cooling equipment. At right, doors 212L and 213L cover the primary hydraulic system (forward) and the left side of the missile auxiliaries bay. The open port, seen in both photos, and marked 210, is for missile bay heating.

WING DETAILS

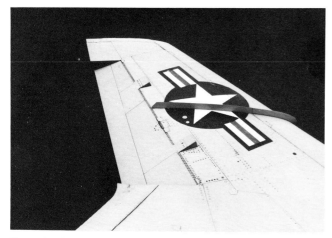

Top of left wing showing aileron detail.

Wing fences on the right wing.

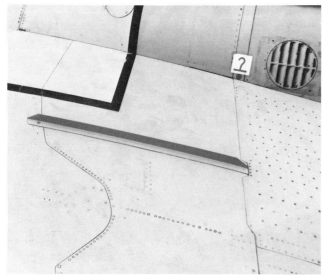

An inner "wing fence" was added to all F-101 versions. Although this may have had some effect on boundary layer air, it was a stiffener for the skin above the wheel well. This was not originally on the F-101.

Close-up view of the boundary layer fence on the left wing.

Left wing fence viewed from the outside.

Small vents were located on top of the wings right next to the fuselage. These were oil cooler air outlets.

WING DATA

Incidence (Root & Tip)	1°
Dihedral	0°
Sweepback (25° Chord)	36° 36'
Area	368 sq ft
Aspect Ratio	4.28
Mean Aerodynamic Chord	122.9 in

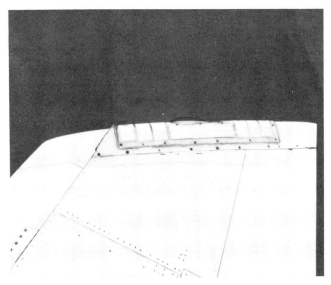

These two photos show the wing tip light layout on the Voodoo. There are the appropriate red or green position lights in the center of the tips, with the pale yellow formation light strips on either side.

Under each wing, next to the fuselage and above the fuel tank connections, is a triangle of four holes, and a larger hole forward of the triangle. The larger hole with the short tube is the wing tank pressure vent. The three small holes in a straight line are the wing tank fuel drains, and the other small hole, next to the three, is the wing tank siphon breaker vent. The photo at left is under the right wing, and the right photo is under the left wing.

Left and right flaps are shown in the lowered position in these photos. The insides of the flaps, and the interior of the flap wells were insignia red, and added color to the aircraft when shown in the lowered position.

SPEED BRAKE DETAIL

All F-101s had speed brakes on the aft fuselage section below the vertical tail. This front view shows the brakes opened to their fullest extent. These speed brakes were also called airbrakes.

Left speed brake in the open position viewed from behind. Note the lightening holes in the brake, and the two holes at the forward end of the well. The interior of the wells and the inside of the brakes were painted insignia red.

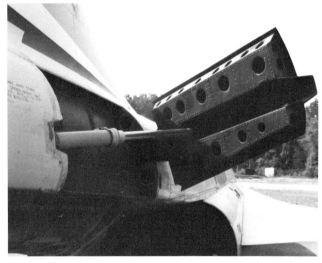

This photo of the right speed brake is included to show the lightening holes in the top of the brake.

Interior of the left speed brake well showing the hydraulic actuating cylinder.

These two photos show more of the details of the right speed brake. Again, note the holes on either side of the hinge in the photo at left, and in the right photo, note the holes in the bottom of the speed brake.(All photos this page Radebaugh)

TAIL DETAILS

The drag chute housing is in the extreme aft end of the tail section. Here a ground crewman is shown repacking the chute.

The right tail formation light panel is visible in this view. It has four segments, and is fifty-four inches long. The little intake slot, between the feathers of the bird, is the bellows flush ram air intake. There is also a small circular intake on the leading edge of the tail, just visible above the top most point of the formation light panel. It is the aft compartment cooling vent.

Fuel vent masts are located on each side of the tail section, just below the rudder. This close-up view reveals good detail of the mast on the left side.

Tail position lights were located under a glass end cap at the aft end of the top tail fairing.

This close-up shows detail of the left side of the horizontal tail hinge. Careful examination of the photograph will reveal graduations marked on the curved portion at the leading edge of the hinge.

Close-up view of the drag chute housing door as viewed from behind and below.

MODELER'S SECTION

KIT REVIEWS

XF-88 KIT

LINDBERG 1/48th SCALE F-88, KIT NUMBERS 509 & 543

Note: This kit was released twice under the two different numbers indicated. Kit number 543 served as a basis for this review, and had features not in Kit 509.

Dating back to the early fifties, this kit comes from the pioneering days of plastic kit manufacturing. The model is advertised to be 1/48th scale, but works out to be about 1/49th in length and 1/47th in span - quite good for a kit from that time period.

The kit is molded in silver plastic, and represents one of the prototypes late in its operational life with the short afterburners and six 20 mm cannon represented. Thus, the model actually represents an XF-88A configuration.

Provided in the kit are forty-eight parts including separate clear canopy and windscreen pieces. The wing tip fuel tanks, once planned for the XF-88, but never used, are also provided. Alternate wing tip pieces are also included, allowing the model to be built in the configuration in which the prototypes actually flew.

On the inside, two ejection seat halves and a pilot make up all there is of a cockpit interior. Top and bottom engine halves, combining both engines, are joined to a forward engine piece for insertion into the fuselage. This prevents the hollow look that was common to many kits of the fifties. There is an "inspection panel" in the top of the left fuselage, and this is best glued into place and the seams sanded out. There are no wheel wells, but the landing gear is quite good, particularly for a kit of this age. A nose test boom is provided, but the small probe under the nose is missing.

Surface scribing is raised for the most part, with control surfaces recessed or provided as separate parts. Scribing, to include rivets, is excellent, and is not overstated. Decals are ficticious, providing no serial number. An "F-88" is on the nose, being shortened from XF-88 as seen on the first prototype.

Although the model has more value to kit collectors, it can be built up into a nice representation of the XF-88A that will fit neatly into any 1/48th scale collection. It may well be one of Lindberg's better kits from the fifties.

Review by Bill Slatton

F-101 KITS

OFF SCALE KITS

MONOGRAM 1/109th SCALE F-101B, KIT NUMBER 6791

With an original copyright release of some twenty-five years ago, this kit does not compare to the Monogram we know today. The kit is in an odd scale, 1/109th as checked by both wingspan and length measurements, and it does not have the extensive detail and attention to accuracy possessed by Monogram's more recent releases.

The general outline is pretty good, but where the kit suffers is lack of detail. There are no boundary layer fences for the wings, no splitter for the intakes, (you can see right through the model and out the exhausts), no strakes along side the missiles, no wing walkways or vents, no cockpit except seats and pilots, and no inner main landing gear doors. The etching for the canopy framing is too swept-back. Decals are of good quality, but very sparse with no particular unit represented.

By adding a lot of missing parts from scratch, a modeler might turn this into a pleasing little representation of the Voodoo, but we doubt that its appeal will be very great to the experienced modeler.

Box art for Monogram's F-101B in 1/109th scale.

REVELL 1/76th SCALE F-101A, KIT NUMBER H-128

Revell claims that this model is 1/80th scale, but measurements indicate that it is more like 1/76th scale. Like the Monogram kit it is quite dated, and it is no longer generally available.

Coming out of the 1950's this kit has all the locations for decals actually etched into the plastic, and the decals themselves are not particularly good. Like the Monogram kit, there are a good number of details missing. Most noticeable of these are the inner doors for the main landing gear and fuel dump masts on the tail. There is one too many external fuel tanks since the F-101 only carried two, but three are provided.

Unlike the Monogram kit, the outline of this kit is not very accurate. Most noticeable are the wingtips, which are too round, the afterburner cans, and the horizontal tail.

The value of this kit lies more with the kit collector than with the model builder who wants a good model of the F-101A/C.

Box art for Revell's 1/76th scale F-101A.

1/144th SCALE KITS

AURORA F-101A, KIT NUMBER 294

This small model also dates back to the fifties, being copyrighted in 1958. It is not actually 1/144th scale, but is fairly close, being just a little large to fit into this "standard" scale size. It measures out to about 1/135th scale. The entire kit is comprised of only fourteen pieces, and that includes the stand!

With no wheel wells, and a rather crude landing gear, the model is best built gear-up on the stand. That reduces to ten the number of parts that will be used. Building the model in this fashion will also require the nose gear doors to be cut off from the two fuselage halves, and the holes for the struts to be filled and sanded. While sanding, the locations for the decals, which are engraved into the plastic, should be removed. The decals do not include a serial number, but buzz numbers FB-419 are included.

A major correction required involves the horizontal stabilizer. It is one piece, and it is perfectly flat. The real thing had a dihedral, so the piece should be cut in half at the centerline, and each side angled up to match the front view drawings shown in this book.

Many details are missing. There is no cockpit, not even a pilot's head. There are no wing fences, no fuel dump masts, no intake ramps, and no probe under the nose. Again, this kit is really one for the kit collectors, and, if built, could only really be made into a small desk stand model.

OTAKI F-101A, KIT NUMBER A-1-100

In outline, this kit represents an F-101A/C fairly well. Where it is lacking is in the detail department. There are no wing fences or stiffeners, no fuel dump masts, no inner main gear doors, no intake ramps or splitter plates, no nose probe, and no cockpit interior. However, in building our review sample, we added all of these features and more using scrap and stock plastic. The effort was really very minimal, took little time, and improved the overall appearance of the model a thousand percent.

Molding of small parts, namely the afterburners and landing gear, leaves a bit to be desired, being inaccurate and incomplete. A little reworking can help, and we suggest replacing all landing gear doors with ones made of thin plastic card. Those in the kit are too thick.

The nose appears a bit too thin when viewed from the side, but just about right when viewed from above. Gun fairings are a little heavy, and should be sanded down a bit.

This may seem like a very critical review, and this kit certainly has its faults. However, with work and detailing, it can be built into a rather nice looking model. We have also seen one converted to an F-101B. The conversion was quite simple, and the results were very pleasing. We recommend giving it a try. If done, the LS Weapons Set in 1/144th scale that includes the AIM-4D Falcons, should be remembered. Addition of the colorful red and white missiles will add a lot to the model. Other conversions to the various reconnaissance versions would also be interesting.

1/72nd SCALE KITS

HASEGAWA/MINICRAFT RF-101A/C, VARIOUS NUMBERS

This kit has been released more times than we care to count. It was also marketed under the Frog name. In each case, the only things changed were the box art, usually the decals, and sometimes the color of the plastic. At any rate, the kit is clearly the better of the two 1/72nd scale models available of the F-101.

The kit is an older release dating back to the 1960's, but it is still a very nice kit. It is accurate in outline and comes with two external fuel tanks. Camera windows are of clear plastic, and the one-piece canopy is both clear and thin. It can easily be cut and opened if desired.

On the short end of the stick, the model lacks a control column and other cockpit detail, in addition to landing lights on the nose gear. The main gear wells are left open

Hasegawa/Minicraft 1/72nd scale RF-101C built stock from the box.

Hasegawa/Minicraft 1/72nd scale RF-101C converted to an F-101B by the author.

Hasegawa/Minicraft 1/72nd scale RF-101C converted to an F-101C.

around the sides, but all of these shortcomings are rather easily rectified to make a super looking model.

Care must be used when assembling the nose gear as the "axle" is offset and one wheel will sit higher than the other unless this error is corrected.

Speed brakes can be positioned open or closed, and this is a nice feature, especially on a camouflaged scheme where the red color of the interior brightens up the otherwise drab appearance of the color scheme.

This model lends itself to easy conversion of an F-101A or -C, and a RF-101G or -H would be equally as easy. A conversion to an F-101B or RF-101B is also possible but would require quite a bit more work. This is a very good kit, particularly considering its age.

MATCHBOX F-101B/F, RF-101B, KIT NUMBER PK-411

This was perhaps one of the most eagerly awaited kits when it was announced, and one of the most disappointing kits when it was released, that we know of. Some of the most obvious detail is missing, and the fit is very poor in general. There are some very important inaccuracies.

The kit is molded in dark green, dark gray, and black -

why? We have no idea. However, the raised scribing is light, and nicely done, much better than in many other Matchbox kits. It is not altogether accurate, but it does not detract from the model the way the deeply recessed scribing in some Matchbox kits does.

There are two nice options offered in this kit that are particularly noteworthy. On the nose, the modeler can select either the IR sensor and fairing, or an open or closed in-flight refueling probe. The doors for the probe are too thick, so if shown in the open position, should be replaced with others made from thin plastic stock. More important, and also on the nose, Matchbox provided the option to build an RF-101B, for which they should be commended. Such options are all too scarce in many kits.

However, we would have given up these options, if there had been any representation whatsoever of the rotary weapons door and missiles. The door is not even scribed into the plastic, let alone being a separate piece. There are no wells for the Falcons nor mounts for the Genies, and no missiles are included in the kit. If the missiles are not carried, a well or something would be visible where they would be mounted. In our estimation, this is inexcusable, and is almost as bad as leaving off a wing!

The main landing gear is incorrect, being for the single seat Voodoos, not the F-101B/F with its wider tires and bulges in the gear doors and under the wings. There is no cockpit detail to speak of, and the noticeable built-up area between the two cockpits is missing.

Ailerons are separate pieces that fit poorly, and must be filled and sanded, then rescribed. Scribing over most fillers does not work well. Fit between the wings and fuselage, in and around the intakes, and under the fuselage, is bad.

Many details are missing, to include the tail hook found on most Voodoos during most of their service life. The identification light and refueling receptacle are represented by decals. Several antennas and upper and lower beacon lights are missing. For the RF-101B, no clear parts are given for the camera windows, black decals being used to represent them instead. Also missing is the air scoop (or slot on early and Canadian CF-101Bs) under the left side of the nose, and the hot air exhaust holes ahead of the missile door. No vortex generators between the exhaust holes and left AIM-4 well are provided. There are no lights on the nose gear, and no nose gear well. Also missing are the data link antennas.

Had this kit come out in the early sixties, some of this lack of detailing would be understandable. (Except for the weapons bay door and missiles.) But this is a kit dated 1980, and by 1980 standards it is very poor.

We purchased several of these kits with one thought in mind - conversion parts. By mating the nose to a Hasegawa kit, the modeler has the makings for an F-101A/C, or with a little more work, an RF-101G/H. We also recommend that such a conversion be done to build an F-101B/F or RF-101B. By using Matchbox parts, such as the nose pieces, burner cans, and scoops, a better model can be built using the Hasegawa kit. In either case, remember to modify the main gear tires, doors, and area under the wings, including the necessary bulges. Also remember to include the air scoop under the nose, and exhaust vents. The "keel" area between the engines and under the tail will also have to be modified on the Hasegawa/Minicraft kit. Gear wells will have to be closed in on the main gear, and don't forget the lights on the nose gear. It's a lot of work, and it would have been nice if the kit provided the basis for a good model. But that is not the case.

There are other problems with the Matchbox kit. Suffice it to say, we find it very disappointing.

1/48th SCALE KIT

MONOGRAM F-101B, KIT NUMBER 5811

The engineering of this kit deserves praise for achieving the massive, involved Voodoo shape in outline, cross-section and detail. Among the many features are complete intake contours all the way back to the compressor blades, the long afterburner cans, detailed inside and out, an intricately molded rotary weapons door with Falcons and Genies, plus a pair of external fuel tanks. Separately molded are flaps, speed brakes, scoops, fuselage strakes, fuel vent masts, and a tail hook. The cockpits are equally well detailed with three-piece seats, instrument panels, flight control column, and an aft side stick for radar control. The excellent clear parts include a gunsight, the windscreen between the two cockpits, the ID light lens, two landing lights and a two-piece canopy with a wet compass molded inside the windshield frame. The canopy has a separate rear bulkhead with storage for a daylight radar scope hood, locating points for two interior rear-view mirrors, and a canopy support strut.

Fit is generally good, but some pre-fitting and trimming is necessary for proper fit for the intakes, cockpit, nose wheel well, landing gear, and weapons door. Otherwise parts fit well, and seams will require a minimum of filling

Monogram's beautiful 1/48th scale F-101B.

(Monogram)

and sanding.

Surface detail is superbly accurate, if lacking in the delicacy of recent imports. Rivets and panel lines are fine, sharp, and raised enough to survive light sanding. The piano hinges on the forward fuselage are over-done, and the formation light panels are raised too much from the fuselage. There are also some molding flaws in the form of dimples on the cooling scoops.

The most obvious error in the kit is the engine bleed louver on the right side which is the same oval shape as the one on the left. It should be rectangular in shape, and some rework will be required here. The engine intake domes should curve outboard facing the incoming air, rather than being straight as Monogram has them.

The praiseworthy engineering of this kit strikes a balance between wealth of detail and practical construction. It builds into an impressive model, and is the best Voodoo kit in any scale.

Review by Warren Munkasy

1/48th SCALE CONVERSION KIT

KOSTER AERO ENTERPRISES KIT NUMBER 10

This kit, designed for use with the Monogram 1/48th scale F-101B, was not available when this book went to press. However, Bill Koster was good enough to provide us with the features of this new kit. By the time this book is published, the kit should be available.

This conversion kit provides the basis for converting the Monogram F-101B into an F-101A/C or RF-101A/C. There are twenty-seven white parts and eight clear pieces. Among the clear parts are RF-101 camera windows and a single seat canopy. White parts include forward fuselage halves, equipment panel, instrument panel and hood, NACA scoop inserts, afterburners, tail pipes, gun fairings, tail "keel" halves, gear doors, wheels, pitot probe, canopy bulkhead, and turbines. In short, this is a complete conversion kit, with all changes taken into consideration, and all necessary parts provided.

This is sure to be a worthwhile kit. It can be ordered from Koster Aero Enterprises, 223 East Ellis Avenue, Libertyville, Illinois 60048. Price is $8.95 including postage.

1/32nd SCALE KIT

COMBAT MODELS F-101, KIT NUMBER 32-032

This vacu-formed kit provides the basis for the only Voodoo model in 1/32nd scale. Being quite large, it comes in a box 12" x 4" x 30", and provides parts to build every version of the F-101. For the most part, it is a matter of

which nose you select, with both types of burner cans also provided. Also included are extremely nice metal landing gear struts, while the wheels are vacu-formed plastic. Two clear canopies, one for the single seat versions, and one for the F-101B/F, are nicely molded, and very clear.

A two-page set of full size plans are included for the RF-101C version only. A third sheet has three views and cross sections for the F-101A, RF-101C, RF-101G, F-101B, and RF-101B. It would have been nice if all of these had been in 1/32nd scale. However, they are slightly smaller than 1/72nd scale. Use of the larger Detail & Scale 1/48th scale drawings will be helpful.

My only complaint about the kit deals with the instructions. The lack of an illustration on the difference in the "keel" area between the engine exhausts was a major omission. However, with the detail photographs now available in this Detail & Scale publication, adequate reference material is available to complete any version. Details on the air scoops for the aft engine compartments, the intake ramps, and the IR fairing were also missing from the instructions, but are provided in this book.

Construction of the model was typical of all large vacu-formed models. There are no complaints here about the fit and construction of the major components. A cockpit tub and seat backs are included that bear a striking resemblance to the Revell 1/32nd F-4 interior! This just cries to be detailed, and as is the case with all vacu-forms, the real challenge is the scratch-building to detail out the cockpits, wheel wells, radars etc, etc, etc. You can go as far as your imagination and skills will allow.

If large scale jets are your thing, then this kit will make a nice addition to your collection.

Review by Don Schmenk

Note: Combat Models is now under a new owner. Their new address is 400 Third Street, West Easton, P.A. 18042.

Combat Models 1/32nd scale vacu-formed kit partly assembled. The various parts and optional noses provided in the kit are shown in this photo. (Schmenk)

DECAL SUMMARY

Note: It is impossible to completely review decals unless the reviewer has actually used the decals on a model to see how they fit. Additionally, markings on a given aircraft can be changed from time to time, so it is possible that the decals may be accurate for one point in time and not another. Therefore, this section is more of a listing of decals available than a review. Review comments are made only in regard to fit when we have actually used the decals or as to accuracy when the evidence clearly indicated an error.

KIT DECALS

1/144th SCALE KITS

Aurora F-101A, Kit Number 294: Contains basic markings only for an aircraft with no serial number. There is a buzz number FB-419, indicating the second F-101A built, 53-2419. No unit markings are provided.

Otaki F-101A, Kit Number A-1-100: Contains only basic markings for F-101A-30-MC, 54-1455. No unit markings are provided.

OFF SCALE KITS

Monogram 1/109th Scale F-101B, Kit Number 6791: Contains only basic Air Force markings, with no unit markings provided.

Revell 1/76th Scale F-101A, Kit Number H-128: Contains basic markings only for the first F-101A-5-MC, 53-2423. No unit markings are provided.

1/72nd SCALE KITS

Hasegawa/Minicraft RF-101C, Various Kit Numbers: As released under the Frog label, markings were provided for two aircraft.
- RF-101C-70-MC, 56-0113, 66th TRW, overall silver
- RF-101C-70-MC, 56-0105, 45th TRS, 460th TRW, AH tail code, 1967, SEA camouflage.

Different releases under the Hasegawa and Minicraft names (Kit Numbers including the digits 037) provided the following markings at various times.
- RF-101C-65-MC, 56-0084, 45th TRS, PACAF, "Polka Dots," overall silver
- RF-101C-60-MC, 56-0054, 15th TRS, PACAF, "Cotton Pickers," overall ADC gray
- RF-101C-65-MC, 56-0066, 45th TRS, PACAF, "Polka Dots," overall silver
- RF-101C-65-MC, 56-0068, 460th TRS, AH tail code, "Mitzie Kay," SEA camouflage
- RF-101C-40-MC, 56-0168, 460th TRS, AH tail code, "Little Miss Sweetness," SEA camouflage

Matchbox F-101B/F, RF-101B, Kit Number PK-411: Contains markings for three aircraft.
- F-101F-86-MC, 57-0307, 178th FIS, North Dakota ANG, "The Happy Hooligans," 1973, ADC gray
- RF-101B, 59-0434, 192nd TRS, Nevada ANG, 1972, SEA camouflage
- CF-101B, 17475, No. 409 "Night Hawk" Squadron, RCAF, overall silver

1/48th SCALE KIT

Monogram F-101B, Kit Number 5811: Contains markings for two aircraft.
- F-101-100-MC, 57-0427, 111th FIS, Texas ANG, "William Tell Champions," overall ADC gray
- CF-101B, 101027, No. 409 "Night Hawk" Squadron, RCAF, overall ADC gray

DECAL SHEETS

1/144th SCALE KITS

Microscale Sheet 14-223: Provides markings for two aircraft.
- F-101A-35-MC, 54-1475, 81st TFW, gray and silver scheme
- F-101A-35-MC, 54-1482, 81st TFW, overall silver

Microscale Sheet 14-247: Provides markings for two aircraft
- F-101C-50-MC, 56-0022, 81st TFW, overall silver
- F-101C-20-MC, 54-1491, 81st TFW, overall silver

Note: These are merely scaled down decals from Microscale's 1/72nd scale sheets 72-223 and 72-247. They were not sized specifically for the Otaki kit, and in many cases, fit is very bad.

1/72nd SCALE SHEETS

Aerodecal Sheet 20A: Contains very sparse markings for four aircraft.
- F-101A-35-MC, 54-1481, 81st TFW, overall silver
- F-101B-105-MC, 58-0302, 132nd FIS, 101st FIG, Maine ANG, "Maine Bangors," overall ADC gray, (*The green pine tree on the tail is misrepresented as blue.*)
- F-101B-105-MC, 58-0274, ADWC, overall ADC gray
- CF-101B, 101054, No. 425 "Alouette" Squadron, RCAF, overall silver

Modeldecal Sheet 10: Provides markings for four different types of aircraft, one of which is RF-101C-75-MC, 56-0119, 45th TRS, 460th TRW, "The Green Dragons," AH tail code, SEA camouflage, in 1969.

Microscale Sheet 72-110: Provides markings for four RF-101Cs.
- RF-101C-70-MC, 56-0101, 363rd TRW, overall silver
- RF-101C-65-MC, 56-0068, 460th TRW, "Mitzie Kay," AH tail code, SEA camouflage
- RF-101C-40-MC, 56-0168, 460th TRW, "Little Miss Sweetness," AH tail code, SEA camouflage
- RF-101C-70-MC, 56-0105, 460th TRW, "The Iron Eyeball," AH tail code, SEA camouflage

Microscale Sheet 72-223: Provides the same markings as Microscale Sheet 14-223 listed above.

Microscale Sheet 72-247: Provides the same markings as Microscale Sheet 14-247 listed above.

Note: Microscale Sheets 72-223 and 72-247 contain conversion parts for converting the Hasegawa/Minicraft RF-101C to an F-101A/C. Nose pieces and gun fairings are included. However the point on the nose is too blunt. We recommend using a nose from a Matchbox kit, but without the static boom.

Microscale Sheet 72-304: Provides markings for three aircraft, one of which is an F-101B-110-MC, 58-0335, in the markings of the 147th FIG, 111th FIS, Texas ANG. The aircraft is in the ADC gray scheme.

Microscale Sheet 72-306: Provides markings for three F-101B/Fs in the earlier overall silver scheme.
- F-101B-100-MC, 57-0431, 61st FIS
- F-101F-106-MC, 58-0262, 4780th Test Squadron, (*Incorrectly listed as an F-101B on the instruction sheets*)
- F-101B-90-MC, 57-0326, 444th FIS

Note: Microscale shows these aircraft to have the IR sensors and fairings on the nose. Our references indicate that these early aircraft did not have them while painted in these colors.

Microscale Sheet 72-307: Provides markings for three F-101Bs in the overall gray scheme.
- F-101B-110-MC, 58-0332, ADWC, 1972
- F-101B-75-MC, 56-0285, 84th FIS
- F-101B-95-MC, 57-0364, 60th FIS, 1965

Microscale Sheet 72-407: Provides markings for three types of aircraft, one of which is F-101B-110-MC, 58-0313, from the 142nd FIG, 123rd FIS, Oregon ANG, in the overall ADC gray scheme.

1/48th SCALE SHEETS

Microscale Sheet 48-263: Provides markings for two aircraft.
- CF-101B, 101043, from the No. 416 "Lynx" Squadron, RCAF, special markings, including a large Lynx and maple leaf, on overall white scheme, 1984
- F-101B-110-MC, 58-0332, Air Defense Weapons Center, overall gray scheme, 1972

Microscale Sheet 48-264: Provides markings for two Canadian Voodoos in unusual markings.
- CF-101B, 101057, No. 409th "Night Hawk" Squadron, in the "Hawk One Canada" scheme, 1984
- EF-101B, 101067, No. 414 "Black Knight" Squadron, in an overall black scheme

Note: The decals listed include all those released as of press time for this book. Since the Monogram 1/48th scale F-101B/F remains a fairly new kit, more sheets are sure to follow. Detail & Scale plans to release at least two sheets for this model.